LIFE IS SWEET...

DESPITE DIABETES!

APARNA VIKRAM JOSHI

INDIA • SINGAPORE • MALAYSIA

ISBN
Paperback 979-8-89588-396-9
Hardcase 979-8-89632-447-8

Index

Preface

It is with a heart full of both love and reverence that I present this book, a tribute to the extraordinary life of my beloved husband.

I am the better half of Vikram Joshi, who has just completed his diamond jubilee birthday on 14th August 2024.

Let me begin by telling you a little about myself:

I am the proprietor of Joshi's Tours & Travels. It's my passion for travelling that got converted into this profession. Travel is more than just visiting new places – it's about creating beautiful memories that last a lifetime. I also take care of the administrative work of Joshi's Investment & Insurance Consultancy where Vikram is the proprietor.

This book, my first attempt to put into words the essence of a man who refused to be defined by his illness, is both a personal journey and a public testament. I have often been asked by many friends and relatives about how he managed to scale mountains, explore unknown areas and face life's challenges head-on while managing a condition where many people find it difficult to cope. The answer lies in his spirit, his resilience, and his refusal to allow anything - least of all diabetes - to stand in his way.

I have written this biography about my husband since I have been a part of his adventurous journey of life. The purpose of sharing his life is that diabetes is a very common disease in today's world. It doesn't show any physical symptoms on the affected person, but it drains the person internally. I see many people taking this disease very casually, which ultimately leads to many serious complications, at a later stage in life.Vikram has lived by the teachings of our guru, our beloved Mahatria. He says that if you land in an ICU because you have not taken care of your health, then you will be lying on the bed with sedatives. But what is the fault of your loved ones who helplessly sit outside the ICU just because they love you? He has taught us to feel responsible for our health and Vikram'sjourney has been nothing short of awe-inspiring!

I feel the way Vikram has taken care of this silent killer disease called diabetes and the way we are living a fabulous life even with a diabetic person at home needs to be shared, because we should be a broadcaster of all the good that happens in your life. In writing this book, I have drawn upon memories and stories from those who knew him the best.

My mentor and guide, Megha Bajaj, who is an award-winning author of many acclaimed books, and founder of WoW (which aids aspiring authors like me to see their dreams come to reality) has guided me by holding my hand. There were many moments where I gave up and told her to carry me on from here; she has always been a very sweet support by giving me new ideas on how I can explore on my own and write further.

Writing this book has been a deeply emotional process, since I went through all our moments together for the last 33 years, which defined the time spent together. I hope you feel one with the tears and smiles.

This is not merely a biography, but a love letter to a man who showed the world that life with diabetes could be lived to the fullest – vibrant, daring, and unapologetic.

May this story inspire others, particularly those facing similar struggles, to see that even in the face of adversity, adventure awaits... to know, life is sweet, despite diabetes!

Aparna Joshi

Foreward

I love making dreams come true for people. Making their thoughts into books - their ideas into a reality.

However, there is one key ingredient I need to do this - and that is Trust.

Aparna came to me with the dream of telling the powerful story of her husband Vikram's journey with Diabetes.

There were so many emotions in her as she expressed to me. I knew this book had to come to life.

The protagonist in Vikram is endearing and yet awe-inspiring.

The story is both relatable and exciting.

Their adventures in Leh, with the careers and especially with Diabetes is a must-read.

However, to me, what stood out the most was the deep love and understanding that Aparna and Vikram share.

This book is more like a love letter written by a wife for her husband, which somehow we all have access to.

Their trials and tribulations, and the way they held onto each other through it all brings a soft smile not just to your face, but to your heart.

I have seen Aparna evolve as a person, as a writer, and even as a mentee.

From having so many doubts, to completely trusting my process - from being so reluctant - to emerging as such a confident storyteller - I can not help but feel both immensely happy and proud of what has been created.

In their story, you will find your own. Especially, if you are a family who is dealing with diabetes -there is so much authenticity, so much courage in this book that you will find it easier to deal with the disease once you have read this.

This book is a testament to true love -of a man for his family, his health and Life,and a woman for her man and his vision.

May it inspire and transform you in the most wonderful ways.

Megha Bajaj

Betselling Author,

Author Mentor and Founder of Wonders of Words (WoW)

Introduction

After completing six decades of his life, at age 60, Vikram is not your average senior. Diagnosed with a disease like diabetes at a very early age of 28, Vikram faced a turning point that could have limited his life and dreams.

Instead, he chose to fight back, transforming his health and embracing every challenge that came his way.

This book chronicles Vikram's incredible journey of overcoming diabetes and embarking on numerous adventures, proving that "AGE" is just a number – it is cour-AGE that defines us, and that life's challenges can be the catalysts for our greatest achievements.

This story is one of resilience, determination, and relentless pursuit of passion. As you turn these pages, you'll be inspired by his unwavering spirit, insightful reflections, and a powerful message that it's never too late to take control of your health and live your dreams.

Join Vikram on this extraordinary journey and discover how overcoming obstacles can lead to a life filled with adventure and excitement.

CHAPTER 1

How You "See" The Disease Makes All The Difference

Something happened three decades ago. There was a young girl, aged 24 by the name Aparna Gajanan Joshi, and a young boy, aged 27 by the name Vikram Vishvanath Joshi. Aparna was working as an assistant in a prestigious organisation called "Unit Trust of India", and Vikram was working in a clerical position in the reputed Nationalised bank "Union Bank of India". The tagline of this bank is "Good People to bank with", and Vikram seemed to live his life by this line.

Aparna was a very shy, introverted girl. She had beautiful brown eyes and thick black hair, but she was very comfortable in her own space and would not like to mingle with many people. She had her own small group where she would let loose and enjoy herself.

Contrary to this, Vikram was a very social person. He would seek opportunities to interact with people. He had the capacity to engage people on various topics like different movies he had seen or the various cuisines he had eaten, etc. He was so friendly with the people whom he worked with that they would be willing to do anything for him, as they found him jovial and pleasant to be around.

It was a typical arranged marriage that brought these two very unlikely people together. Aparna's parents were non-believers in horoscope matching. However, Vikram's parents were in favour of matching horoscopes. Now, there was a twist here. The horoscopes were matching with only three points. However, it was suggested to Vikram's parents by the astrologer who was a friend of Vikram's father that Aparna was the perfect match for their son since she had very good compatibility with him. Reluctantly, a meeting was set.

It was Aparna and her parents who went to Vikram's house, which was at Vile Parle, Mumbai –Parle Nimesh society. The house had two entrances since it was on the ground floor. In those days, the boy and girl were not allowed to meet in person initially. It was through the medium of photographs to decide if the boy or girl was a match. Vikram, along with his friends, was standing outside the gate, hiding himself amongst his friends.

This was his tactic to see the girl and decide if she was fit to be his wife. The moment he saw Aparna get out of the autorickshaw, he told his friend, "She is the girl I would be willing to marry. She completely fits into my imagination of a wife." After Aparna and her parents entered the house, this fellow slowly (and slyly) came from the backdoor and sat in front of everyone with a very innocent face as if seeing her for the first time. For Aparna also, it so happened that it was love at first sight. They had a very big house, and Vikram also had light brown eyes and looked very handsome. Also, Vile Parle was just the next station to Andheri, and Aparna also made up her mind that Vikram was the right choice for her. So now, despite the horoscope (horror-scope), the girl, and the boy were all ready for this marriage.

Thus, on 25th May 1991, these two souls embarked on a journey that would intertwine their lives in a bond of love and commitment. In that moment, amidst the celebration, little did they know about the various challenges that would test the very foundation of their union and gift them with adventures that could be made into a book!

I, Aparna Joshi, at age 55, decided that the last few decades of our life were so full of experiences and learnings that they had to be documented. So here I am, writing this book for all of you – to tell you the story of "US" which will reveal how we both, through resilience, love, and unwavering support, overcame all the obstacles together, holding hands together.

The initial days of our marriage were rosy days, and we enjoyed our life a lot. As I have already mentioned, our home in Vile Parle had two entrances: one was the main entrance to the living room, and one was from our bedroom. We used to go see movies after dinner, and Vikram's parents wouldn't know since it was a backdoor entrance. At that time, we used to find it thrilling to do such small acts of rebellion and mischief and gain immense happiness out of it. Because of my shy nature, I once asked Vikram, "What will happen if we get caught by your parents? They might think we are sleeping in our bedroom." To this, Vikram smiled and replied, "My parents know me very well, and they will not be surprised to see that I have taken my wife for a movie or to eat ice cream through this backdoor of our house. I have been a mischievous child throughout my childhood and continue to be..." I could only smile in agreement.

A beautiful anecdote from these days comes to my mind. Those days, having an AC car was a luxury, and Vikram's friend Nitin Kushe (who is no longer alive) had this car. Once we decided to go to Lonavala at 7 pm. So, we both, his other friend Sachin and his wife Pradnya, and this Nitin, we left for Lonavala at 7 pm. At that time, there was no expressway. We had to go via Khandala ghat. The car suddenly stopped at one of the turns in the ghat. We were very much in the middle of the ghat, and it was 10.30 pm.

We all got scared, but to our surprise we found a mechanic. He said we would have to go all the way down to get the car repaired. The mechanic asked us, "Who can ride my scooter down the ghat so that I can bring this car down only with the help of this slope of the ghat?" Vikram had learned to ride a Bajaj scooter, so it was decided that Vikram would ride the scooter all the way back in the Khandala ghat. The mechanic just took the car down the ghat using his mechanical skills. My attention was fully on how Vikram would bring the scooter down the ghat. It was very dark, and no streetlights guided him. It was a very scary situation for him. The lights coming from the vehicles in the opposite direction were very disturbing. They would directly hit his eyes, and it was difficult to find the road ahead.

Somehow, he managed to come down the ghat. It took almost an hour for the mechanic to repair the car, and then we started our journey back to Lonavala. What was incredible through it all was, that though I was nervous, Vikram remained smiling throughout.

I think this was a clue that our life was going to be full of adventures.

The whole family was overjoyed when they came to know that we both were on the way to becoming three of "US." On 2nd July 1992, the world heard a cry it had never heard before. This cry was of our bald, very fair, and blue-eyed son. "ROHAN," we named him. The joy of holding him in our arms was boundless and we were filled with gratitude and grace. Our life had turned in a 180-degree angle, and we were busy day and night with the schedule of this little boy. On the fourteenth day, Rohan fell so sick that he had to be admitted to Nanavati Hospital. It was a dreadful night for us. It was raining heavily, and because of my C-section, I could not go to the hospital. It was my father-in-law and my parents who went to admit Rohan. For this incident, I am ever grateful to my father-in-law. The hospital asked for a deposit of Rs. 6000, and if they would not pay, they would not be able to admit the little child. At that time, there was no card system or ATM or G-pay. But my father-in-law put his gold ring in front of them and asked them to admit the baby. The hospital authorities were speechless, and they admitted Rohan immediately and started the necessary treatment. (It sounds almost like a scene from a movie, but to know how deeply we were all loved, and protected – this incident has to be shared!)

For the next 24 hours, Vikram was just sitting next to him in the hospital. I had no other option but to pray. God came in the form of Dr. Rashid Merchant, who happened to be the husband of Vikram's officer, Mrs. Suraiya Merchant. He gave us our Rohan once again, a healthy and happy baby. He also told us that the baby was really in a bad state, and hence we should celebrate his birthday from that day.

After this big incident, we thought life had come back to normal. But as they say, life is a journey of twists and turns. Fate had other plans in store for us. Here we had a big twist in our life. Vikram, who was a very healthy person, suddenly started losing weight drastically and became very lethargic. He had reduced from 70 kg to 56 kg.

Here again, I feel immense gratitude to my father-in-law. One fine evening, when he returned from work, he got angry to see Vikram sleeping in the evening. This used to happen very often. But that day he woke up Vikram and told him, "Look Vikram, I am seeing that you are getting too tired after working in the bank and you have also lost a lot of weight. This is not a good sign at such a young age. Get ready and I am going to take you to visit Dr. Vijay Parulekar immediately."

Dr. Parulekar was a very senior General Surgeon and a good friend of my father-in-law. Just looking at Vikram, he sensed something fishy and asked him, "Why did you wait for so long?"

A few tests were done, and all of us were very nervous as the results were awaited. I could not fathom why such a healthy man had suddenly become so lethargic and seemed to not be himself at all.

Finally, the blood tests revealed that his sugar levels had gone up to 500, which was very alarming. Type 1 "DIABETES" was detected in a young 28-year-old who had just taken the responsibility of a wife and a son upon his shoulders. There was no family history for this disease. As a family, we all were in a state of shock and disbelief. We were asked to meet Dr. Ajgaonkar, who was a very well-known diabetologist. On our very first visit to Dr. Ajgaonkar, Vikram was put on "INSULIN" injections for a lifetime.

TYPE-1 diabetes is a disease where the functioning of the pancreas of the person slows down drastically. Unlike type-2 diabetes, which often develops due to lifestyle factors, type-1 diabetes is primarily an autoimmune condition. The treatment for this type of diabetes is only the insulin therapy. The blood sugar levels need to be monitored because the insulin-dependent diabetic patient may also go into hypoglycaemia if the sugar level drops drastically. Despite diligent management, individuals with Type-1 diabetes are at risk for long-term complications, including cardiovascular diseases, nerve damage, and eye damage. In short, Vikram had come in the category of "LADA" patient. The full form of which is Latent Autoimmune Diabetes in Adults.

Vikram's stressful nature was the cause behind this effect. His major stress was that he had lost a lot of money in the Harshad Mehta scam. Vikram, being an introverted person, had not vented out his tension with anyone, not even with me. Vikram and I literally cried our hearts out that night. The very thought of taking insulin for a lifetime was scary, and Rohan was hardly 4 months old. My initial shock now began to subside, and a feeling of responsibility took over me of supporting dear Vikram through this challenging phase of life.

And now, at Vikram's age 60, when we look back, we feel we have come such a long way. Without hampering any other body parts (which usually happens in many diabetic patients) and living a very disciplined life, along with all the adventurous things that we did, I really feel this journey of "US" needs to be shared with people and let them know that if you treat diabetes as your "friend", it will not trouble you. It will walk the path along with you but silently. They say diabetes is a silent killer, but if you handle this friend with care, it will allow you to live your life as you had envisioned it, without getting into the way. How you "SEE" the disease makes all the difference!

Read on to know what happened next...

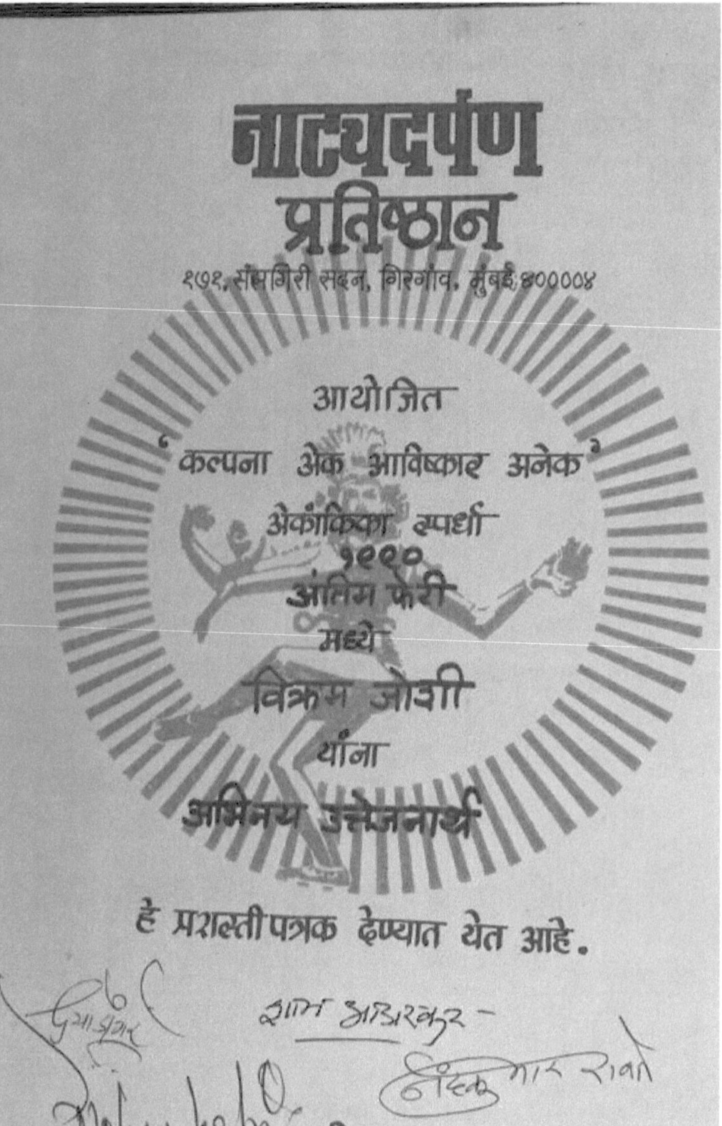

नाट्यदर्पण
प्रतिष्ठान
१७१, संमगिरी सदन, गिरगांव, मुंबई ४००००४

आयोजित
'कल्पना ऐक आविष्कार अनेक'
ऐकांकिका स्पर्धा
१९९०
अंतिम फेरी
मध्ये
विक्रम जोशी
यांना
अभिनय उत्तेजनार्थ

हे प्रशस्ती पत्रक देण्यात येत आहे.

परिक्षक

Banks' Sports Board

XIII All India Inter-Bank Drama Competition
2001-2002

Organised by :

punjab national bank

Head Office : 7 Bhikhaiji Cama Place,
New Delhi-110 066

CERTIFICATE

This is to certify that Mr./~~Ms.~~ VIKRAM JOSHI

Participated in XIII All India Inter-Bank Drama Competition, 2001-2002 held at Pyare Lal Bhawan, Bahadur Shah Zafar Marg, New Delhi-110002 from 30th October, 2001 to 04th November, 2001.

He/she represented UNION BANK OF INDIA

and secured III place in the Best Actor

C. K. D. Gowda
Dy. General Manager - H.R.D.
Punjab National Bank, H.O. New Delhi

Dated : 04th November, 2001

PARLE TILAK VIDYALAYA ASSOCIATION'S

M. L. Dahanukar College of Commerce - Junior College

BOMBAY-400 057

GYMKHANA

CERTIFICATE OF PROFICIENCY

This is to certify that

SHRI. VIKRAM V. JOSHI

of F. Y. J. C. was/~~XXXX~~ declared SECOND

in C A R R O M MEN'S SINGLES

at the Annual Sports of the College held during the year 19 79 - 19 80.

Principal.

~~In-Charge~~

Physical Education,

CHAPTER 2

If You Know The "Why" You Will Never "Cry"

So, now, from the year 1992 onwards, a new adventure journey started for us. Our life suddenly started revolving around blood sugar levels, medication, and lifestyle changes. During those times, there was no Google for us to gain some extra knowledge on this subject. The only Google available was our parents, and they were very supportive. There is a profound impact of family support during such challenging times.

It is during such critical junctures that the true strength and resilience of family bonds shine the brightest. My uncle, aunt, Vikram's brother, and sister-in-law (Vivek and Swati), my sister Ashwini, all of them cocooned us with their love, warmth and understand - the moral support which was really required at that point of time. My younger sister Ashwini was already studying medicine at GS Medical College, KEM Hospital.

Vikram's mother and my mother were the first ones to tell us not to panic. They said, let us study about this diabetes and plan

Vikram's meal accordingly. His brother Vivek said that he had read somewhere that exercise helps to reduce sugar. He asked Vikram, "Hey bro, how about going for evening walks together?" His father was the strongest support. He told Vikram, "My dear son, this is a sudden shift in your health condition. But remember one thing, that you are not alone. The whole family, as a team, shall figure it out along with you step by step."

My personality was completely opposite to my sister's. I just could not stand the atmosphere of a hospital, nor could I see anyone in pain. But here I was, with my husband diagnosed with insulin-dependent diabetes, and I had to give him that insulin injection on his arms daily. With every prick, it really used to hurt me mentally. But we both decided to be strong and hold each other's hand till the end. Here, I told Vikram that he was not alone in this journey and that I shall be his support in every step of life.

There is one instance which really stands out in my memory. Vikram has a sweet tooth. He loved to eat sweets and here he was, diagnosed with diabetes where eating sweets is considered as poison. Rohan was too small to understand what exactly had happened to his father. He only understood that his father can't eat sweet things though he likes sweets a lot. So, he once told me, "Aai, we shall eat ice cream only when we both go out. If we bring ice cream home and eat, baba will feel bad." At that moment, tears trickled down my eyes and I was so touched to see little Rohan's reaction to all this. Also, those days, we both were hardcore atheists and hence we did not go to any temple to seek God's help. We had confidence that we can manage it on our own.

During those times, whenever I used to see my friends, relatives enjoying their life hale and hearty, I would feel frustrated that why such a disease struck my husband only! Why so? Of course, we both were too young to get an answer to this. Now, when I heard from my Guru Mahatria, he says, in life, if you know the "WHY", you will never "CRY". I now understand that each of us del with our own destiny, our own share of highs and lows and going through it with dignity and grace is the only answer.

Vikram had only two best friends, Sachin Sinkar and Nitin Kushe. They both had individual cars at that time, and we did not even have a two-wheeler, nor could we afford it at that time. I started getting driven by such aspirations and societal pressures. Also, the responsibility of Rohan's education started worrying me. So, one day, I had a big fight with Vikram and demanded that I also want some luxuries in our life. I screamed, "Because of your diabetes, you cannot make any additional income. You get exhausted just with your job in Union Bank of India." I even asked him, "When you sit in the car with Nitin, don't you get the feeling that I should also have a car of my own?"

Vikram looked at me startled as till then he had only seen a very supportive wife. But I was completely upset that evening and said, "I am really feeling suffocated since we do not have enough money for luxuries."

Today, when I think of that evening, I really feel ashamed of myself and regret what I said. Vikram was suffering from a disease even though he had not done anything wrong. From my today's maturity, I do understand that it was the immaturity of that age and that Aparna was fighting with him.

On the contrary, Vikram took my harsh words very seriously and promised himself that he would try to do something after office hours. He started doing small businesses like selling crackers during Diwali time, mangoes during the mango season, etc. One fine day he realized that he could be a good teacher, and he could take tuition. This realization was from his college days. He had taught Math to one of his cousins, Abhay, who was poor in the subject. And because of Vikram's teaching, he had cleared the exam with decent marks.

So, now he started his teaching with one student. He used to teach all Commerce subjects. His proficiency was that he was not teaching the bright scholars to get centum, but he was teaching such students who were finding it difficult to even clear an exam, and Vikram was helping them to clear the exam with quite decent marks. I still remember the joy on a mother's face when her son had "passed" his exam with good marks. This spread among the child's friends and Vikram had some more students.

Our bedroom would be converted into a classroom in the evening. Since we were living in a joint family, and Vikram's parents were also working, It was really a challenging job to conduct classes at home. But Vikram was managing it very well, since he had promised his wife that he would generate some more income than only a salary. Slowly, he shifted the classes to the students' home, which was a bungalow in Juhu. But then he also realized that if we have our own space for taking tuitions, that would be a good solution. My office was giving us a home loan at a very decent rate. We grabbed this opportunity and purchased a small ownership office in Vile Parle. What a proud feeling it was for both of us! From where to where – despite the adventures...

It was through this phase that my admiration and respect for Vikram really started to grow. I saw how versatile he was and how anything he took up, he did very well and excelled at it. Along with work, being a husband, parent, and son – and managing small jobs to earn extra, Vikram surprisingly managed to keep his hobbies and passion alive.

He had inherited the quality of acting from his father. Hence, he used to participate in all the Inter Bank Drama competitions and would win various prizes for his bank. He has many awards to his credit. But all these competitions used to happen in Mumbai only. Once he was to participate in All India Inter Bank Competition which was to be held at Indore. Now I started worrying and asked him, "Vikram, I feel you should not go out of Mumbai for this competition. How are you going to manage your insulin schedule?"

Vikram, however, had answers to all my questions. He said, "Aparna, this competition is very important since I represent my bank. Don't worry about my schedule. I will take care of myself." For this competition, he had to go out of Mumbai for many days at a stretch. Reluctantly, I agreed to his Indore tour. All those days, I kept worrying about how he must be managing his schedule. Today, we communicate with each other so easily. During those days, communication was not so easy. He brought a lot of happiness and great news for all of us when he came back. His health was totally fine, and he had bagged the "Best Actor" award. So, his bank management was also very happy. Vikram was also good at playing carom. He has won many prizes for carom as well.

However, as time progresses, with perseverance and determination, even the most daunting paths can gradually ease into a more manageable and fulfilling experience. Vikram started focusing on healthy eating. He has a very sweet tooth, but if anyone would offer him any sweet, he would very reluctantly avoid having it. I saw my husband grow in so many areas – and along with him kept growing my love and respect for this man who did everything he could, despite diabetes. I saw him as an inspiration for many others.

CHAPTER 3

If You Want Something In Life, The Whole Universe Conspires For You To Get It

As the journey unfolds, small victories emerge, and each one is a testament to the strength of character and unwavering resolve. As time passes, the once-daunting journey begins to take on a new hue.

It took a lot of perseverance, determination, and a shared vision – but finally, we started seeing a green patch in our life. Money started coming in, and our lifestyle started improving. This was exactly 3 years after our engagement. I will never forget that special date when the blue beauty entered our life. Yes, a Kinetic Honda scooter became a part of our beautiful family on 6th April 1994. By now, it was clear that though we did not have the full money to buy a scooter, we could easily afford an EMI. So, we approached a bank, and with the loan offered, we could easily take this Kinetic Honda.

With this small achievement, we were on cloud nine, utterly jubilant. We would travel anywhere now with our scooter. We travelled on it as far as Borivali, Chembur, Vashi, and our joy was immeasurable. Vikram's father was very reluctant and would scold us that we should not take Rohan with us on long rides. But since we were young and adventourous, we would convince him that we will ride very carefully, and we trio would go everywhere. Today when we see people taking their children on two wheelers, we get scared and empathize with the concern of Vikram's father at that time.

On one of our rides to the National Park - Borivali, Rohan's cap just flew away from his head, and he started crying that his cap had flown away. Sitting behind, I also started looking back and shouting that the cap was flying away. Vikram took the scooter to the side of the road, and we both got a lot of firing from him. He scolded us, saying, "Why are you both shouting for the silly cap which flew away? If I lose control of the scooter because of your anxiety, just imagine what will happen. Our lives are more important than the cap. I have promised my father that I shall ride safely, so please don't get excited about such silly things. Let the cap go; we shall buy a new one." But everything had happened in such a fraction of a second that it was an instant reaction of Rohan and me and today we can only laugh together at the incident and I can still visualize that cap flying and Vikram scolding!We had not only achieved our initial goal of having some extra income but were thinking of exceeding it by starting a full-fledged class. However, Vikram had a permanent job in a bank, and at that point leaving the existing job would not be a good alternative.

By this time, my father was on the verge of his retirement. My mother had taken up agencies of various investments like post office, fixed deposit, etc. But now, when my father was retiring from his office, she decided to surrender her agencies. It was a very small business which she was doing with very few known clients. Vikram, being a versatile individual, saw an opportunity for himself to leverage his skills and talents.

He just happened to ask my mother if he would take up her small empire? By doing small part-time businesses, he got a little entrepreneurial spirit in him. He was confident that he would build something good on the foundation laid by my mother. My parents immediately agreed to this. So, Vikram first completed the syllabus of his existing students and now started this investment business, which he could easily do after office hours.

The investment business which Vikram had taken up had made a decisive shift from our past and had set the stage for a new direction in life. When Vikram was going through these changes in life, I was more involved in my own service at Unit Trust of India, and I was busy taking care of Rohan. Those were his growing years and I wanted to do justice. Hence, I was not involved in Vikram's business. He could also do it in his part-time, so in whatever small way I could help him, I was doing. But this phase of life was very hectic for both of us.

In all this, we can't forget his diabetes. By this time, his fluctuations in sugar level continued. Every six months we had to visit Dr. Ajgaonkar. He would address Vikram as "RAJE", which means a "King", because, though his sugar levels were fluctuating, Vikram would always greet the doctor with a smiling face.

During these times, we were managing Vikram's diabetes very mechanically. My role had become that of a nurse who would remind him of his insulin in his hectic schedule.

However much you try to control this disease called Diabetes, it is still considered a silent killer. There is one incident that needs to be shared.

The first organ that diabetes attacks is the feet of the person. So, Vikram started experiencing a lot of pain in his legs, and they looked reddish. We went to Dr. Pravin Kothari (he is no longer alive), who was a very good physician and a good friend of my younger sister. He called us at Sanjeevani Hospital at Andheri, and looking at Vikram's legs, he asked us to get him admitted. Vikram was not at all ready to get admitted and was almost on the verge of running away. Here, my sister Dr. Ashwini explained to him why hospitalization was necessary and convinced him to get admitted. Within 4 days, he was once again hale and hearty. Our learning here was, diabetes needs good medical care and proper rest and one needs to ensure that this is gifted to the body so it can function well despite the disease.Now during these 4 days, he was given all the diet food. But this diet food was tasty. Vikram called upon the chef of the hospital and appreciated him a lot for the food he was serving the patients. This chef was so overwhelmed; he said that Vikram was the first patient who called him to appreciate the diet and bland food that was served to the patient.

So, this is Vikram, who, though being hospitalized as a patient, maintained his positive attitude and gratitude despite the challenging circumstances.

If you decide something very sincerely, the world conspires to get you what you want. Similarly, Vikram happened to meet Mr. Shashank Bawkar, who was a Development Officer in LIFE INSURANCE CORPORATION OF INDIA. The moment he came to know that Vikram had taken up part-time investment agency business, he started insisting Vikram to take up an LIC agency in the name of my mother and do the insurance business simultaneously. This is something for which he faced a lot of rejection from me and both our parents. One thing was that the insurance agency would require a lot of attention, and I was not in favour of going to anyone asking for an insurance policy. Also, during those times, an insurance agent was not respected at all; it was not considered a dignified profession. Little did I know that insurance would be our main profession in the future.

But, as Development officers can motivate you until they succeed, so did Mr. Shashank Bawkar. One evening when we were discussing whether to take up this insurance agency, Vikram told me, "Aparna, don't look at this profession only from the business perspective. This is the only profession which gives financial security to the entire family if something goes wrong with the breadwinner. Just imagine what the family would feel if we gave them their insurance claim if they lose their main breadwinner."

When we all looked from this angle, we thought this was a good profession and one fine day, Vikram took my mother to the LIC office and with some formalities, she became an insurance agent with LIC of India. Here, of course, a big salute to my mother, who supported her son-in-law at that time. From here onwards, we boarded the Rajdhani Express of our life journey.

This was like setting sail into the unknown. The investment business which we were already doing was just like helping clients to keep their money in safe instruments which were already available on the market. Selling an insurance policy was not that easy. We had to emphasise the importance of protecting individuals and families from unforeseen risks like sudden death of the breadwinner or any permanent disability that would be in the family and self-retirement. So, some guidance was required.

Our Development Officer, Mr. Shashank Bawkar, immediately suggested an institute called "Indian Institute of Excellence" which was providing training to Insurance Agents. Vikram started attending various training sessions at this institute. They offered a lifetime course called the "Commitment Course". The cost of the course was Rs. 1,50,000/-. At the time in 2002-2003, this was a significant investment amount for us, and hence we were both reluctant. However, our Development Officer inspired us to a point where we felt compelled to invest this significant amount in our own growth and development, knowing that it would lead to our personal and professional advancement.

Vikram's diabetes was more related to stress, and this was too much of a stress for him, and his sugar levels started fluctuating. By this time, I had a big realization that prioritizing health was more important than just chasing behind wealth. While financial success is important, it pales in comparison to the value of maintaining good health. But you never know what the future has in store for you!

As they say, "When the student in you is ready, the right teacher or guru comes in search of you." Here is when we met our first guru in life, Mr. Deipakk Josshi, whom we refer to as Dipakk bhai. He came into Vikram's life as a professional guru, as well as a Life Guru. Vikram started attending the institute's commitment course, which used to start exactly at 7.00 am every Wednesday morning at City Point Hotel, Dadar. This course continues to be an integral part of our life even after so many years. Our Deipakk bhai's vision was that a mother should proudly tell her child to take up the profession of an insurance agent. Till that time, this profession was not considered a very good profession. It used to be the last option for a person who was left with nothing else to do.

Deeipakk bhai's teaching was that you earn money in the right way and increase your standard of living. An old saying goes, "chaddar dekh ke haat pair failao." This was reversed by him by teaching us "tum haat pair failate jaao, chaddar apne aap fail jayegi." "Dreams come true" is what he would imbibe. Of course, all of this is what Vikram used to share with me. But we both would wonder whether this can really be true. Is it practical? He would say, if you dream "nothing," "nothing" will come true.

Here, I would quote another guru, my beloved "Mahatria," because at this moment his quote was coming true.

"A time comes in the life of a caterpillar when he doesn't want to be a caterpillar anymore, and this is the beginning of a butterfly. Somewhere in the life of a human being, a time must come when you are ready to draw a line to your past and get futuristic to the objectives of your life." I think this was the time in Vikram's life when he was getting continuous inspiration from Deipakk bhai to earn good money. Of course, this was going on along with his job intact in the bank.

CHAPTER 4

Dreams Come True

One fine day, Vikram was going with his friend Nitin Kushe in his car. We Parlekars live close to the airport, which allows us to have a very close view of landing flights. The runway being very close to us, the landing flights fly over our buildings.

That day, the "Alitalia" airlines flight was landing, and Vikram told his friend, "Nitin, looking at this landing flight, a thought flashed through my mind. I feel that I should take Aparna and Rohan on a vacation to Europe." Nitin immediately replied, "Hey Vikram, if you decide, you can easily achieve it. What you need for a vacation in Europe is just some extra money." A strong desire filled Vikram's heart. Here again, as my Guru Mahatria would say, Vikram was standing on 'reality' that we did not have enough money to go on a Europe tour but was focusing on a "desire" to celebrate our 12th Wedding anniversary in Switzerland.

In life, there are moments when our deepest desires seem like distant fantasies or mere whispers of possibility in the vast expanse of the unknown.

He came and shared this desire with me, and I literally laughed at him, thinking that he had gone completely mad. I reminded him and told him, "Hey dear hubby, whatever you are saying is exciting, but it can't come true. Just remember we both are clerks in our respective organisations." I had many doubts in my mind. Would we ever be able to afford such an expensive tour? Do we even have the courage to embark on this grand adventure? We did not even have our passports." Through this whirlwind of my doubts and fleeting moments of uncertainty, Vikram remained steadfast in his pursuit, drawing strength from his unwavering belief in the power of his dreams.

For me, this was a dream which I thought was impossible and hence I was not of any help to him as related to the business that he was doing. But Vikram, on the other hand, with the guidance of our Guru Deipakk bhai, managed to slog a lot by selling insurance after office hours, and thereby he earned so much that we three were booked on an 18-day Europe tour along with London. The cost of the tour was Rs. 1,35,000 per person and for Rohan it was Rs. 70,000. I am quoting the price here especially because this was the same Vikram who was reluctant to pay Rs.1,50,000 for a lifetime training. We went on this tour with Edu International. The proprietors of this tour agency were Mr. and Mrs. Shinde.

I still remember the day we were supposed to leave for this international tour. I was feeling so proud of my better half, who had managed to earn enough money to take both of us on an international holiday all the way to Europe. And the miracle was that we were to board our "Alitalia" flight to Rome. This was our first international experience, and Rohan was very excited. He kept on telling me, "Aai, apan desh sodun challo."

The moment the flight took off, I held Vikram's hand tightly. It was a momentous occasion, filled with a complex array of emotions. Some things go well unsaid. I had a sense of pride and accomplishment. On 25th May 2003, we were in Austria at Swarovski. As promised, Vikram had made his dream come true by celebrating our 12th wedding anniversary in Europe. This tour was again a big turning point in our life.

By this time, the organization in which I was working, Unit Trust of India, was on the verge of closure. The government had decided to liquidate UTI, so we were given a chance to opt for voluntary retirement. Here, I will share some of the incidents of our tour. Our tour guide, Mr. Porus, made our tour joyful by narrating so many interesting things about the history of different countries. It was so mesmerizing to see the Eiffel Tower, and when we reached the third level of the Eiffel Tower, we literally understood the meaning of what it is to be "ON TOP OF THE WORLD."

The gondola ride in Venice can never be forgotten because we both loved the song, "do lafzon ki hai, dil ki kahani" ... which is picturized here. This again was one more experience of dreams coming true. Disneyland made us go back to fairy tale days, rather it was like "Alice in Wonderland." During the entire journey of 18 days, Vikram was very cautious in taking care of his diabetes, taking insulin regularly, and that's why we could enjoy our tour thoroughly.

Finally, we departed from the tour in London at one of my aunt's houses whose name is Vidya Godbole (who is no longer alive). Vikram was meeting her for the very first time, but she and her son Kedar were such lovely hosts; we enjoyed our stay in London. We went to see "Lords," where India had won our first World Cup.

Now, why am I saying this tour was a turning point is that both Mr. and Mrs. Shinde were motivating us continuously throughout the tour to join them in their profession of travel tourism. Mrs. Shinde was a schoolteacher and Mr. Shinde a professor in college. But they both were conducting international tours twice every year during the vacations.

Now, there were two options in front of me. Since UTI was on the verge of closure, every person in the organisation was tense. 'To Be or Not To Be?' was a million-dollar question for everyone. We all were in our mid-thirties, and it was a very tricky situation. But by now, I had tasted the sweet fruit of the insurance profession, and this tourism profession was also lingering in my mind. It was really a tough time; Rohan was studying in std 6th. Here again, Vikram became a big supporter and asked me to opt for the voluntary retirement, to which I agreed immediately.

My decision to embrace VRS was not triggered by dissatisfaction but was rather driven by a desire for growth and reinvention.

CHAPTER 5

This and That

After dedicating fourteen years of my life to Unit Trust of India, it was time for a change in life. In the context of Ramayana, I had completed my exile. But the journey of working with a reputed organization like UTI was a great experience. I had learned so many new things in life. I was fortunate to get an opportunity to work on a computer at a time when computers were not as popular as they are today. I had many friends in UTI. We used to travel by train to Churchgate daily. Travelling on Mumbai local trains itself teaches you so much in life. My heart ached to leave my organization mid-way, but I had no regrets because a strong hand called "Vikram" was there to lead my life further.

Leaving my job marked the beginning of a transformative journey – a journey that led me to spread my wings and embrace the freedom of entrepreneurship. Leaving the security of a steady paycheck behind was daunting yet liberating.

It opened a realm of possibilities and opportunities waiting to be explored.

I started studying for the IRDA exam and after clearing the same, I took up the LIC agency in my name. Now, willingly, I started going with Vikram to the commitment course every Wednesday. Here again, the versatile Vikram told me, "We should do THIS and THAT." So, he asked me to contact Madam Shinde, and I started canvassing people that I am also in the international tourism profession. I managed to get four of my friends who willingly joined me for a tour to Thailand, Malaysia, and Singapore with Edu International, guided by Mrs. Shinde.

When the departure day drew closer, I was filled with a mix of excitement and dread. I was scared to leave Vikram and Rohan alone at home, since Rohan was too young and was not sure how Vikram would manage his diet and insulin. The thought of him managing everything on his own was unnerving. But Vikram did not utter a single negative sentence. He gave me so much confidence that he would manage his health well. Despite his reassurances, I couldn't shake off the worry that something might go wrong in my absence.

The day of departure was bittersweet. As I boarded the plane, I couldn't help but feel a pang of guilt. Was I being selfish by leaving both at home alone? Such questions kept lingering in my mind until the plane took off. But when I returned from this tour, I was very happy to see Vikram hale and hearty. He had kept his promise and had managed his diet well as well as his insulin.

Vikram being Vikram, now a new thought started lingering in his mind. After my first tour, he started saying that we should start this profession on our own because he had a strong feeling that if people travel with us for 10-12 days, they will get to know us very well and they might come to us for their investments. Since the insurance and investment profession is totally based on 'trust' and vice versa, those who were already our investment clients would love to travel with us on an international holiday.

At first, I was hesitant. The tourism industry is very competitive and unpredictable. The idea of starting our own tourism profession seemed daunting. But Vikram's unwavering belief in our abilities and his infectious enthusiasm gradually began to erode my doubts. I called up Shinde madam to tell her, and she was happy to know that I was so inspired that we took the decision to start our own tourism profession.

So, 2004 was the beginning of "Joshi's tours and travels." Our first customers obviously were my parents, my friends, and relatives. So, our first tour to Thailand, Singapore, Malaysia was a grand success. But again, to get new people for our newly set profession was difficult. If we declared the tour and were falling short of people, we would get sleepless nights. Again, with so much stress, Vikram's sugar levels started fluctuating.

But now, from 1992 to 2004, diabetes had become a good friend of Vikram. Diabetes itself by now came to know that he had a brave friend called Vikram. As goes his name, Vikram means "valorous"...one who is wise, brave, and strong as well as victorious.

Here I would love to quote an incident from my second tour of Singapore, Thailand, Malaysia.

A few years back, there was a requirement that if a person was not a graduate, a stamp "ECNR" was compulsory on their passport when they flew to countries like Singapore, Thailand, and Malaysia.

In our very second tour, there was a family and their young daughter's passport was stamped "ECNR," but the word "Thailand" was not written on it. We were taking a group of forty passengers with us. It was a day flight of Singapore Airlines. At the immigration counter, the officer refused to allow this girl to proceed. We were totally panicked as to what could be done.

The officer suggested that you go to Santacruz where this procedure is done, get the word Thailand written on it, and get it stamped. It was really a very tough situation; the remaining thirty-six passengers had already done with the immigration process.

Within a fraction of a second, Vikram said that he would rush to Santacruz and get it done. I was totally panicked. It was a very fragile situation. We could not leave that family alone, nor could we let the other passengers go without us. But Vikram literally rushed to Santacruz and got the procedure done, came back to the airport totally panting for breath. He had to literally leave the auto midway since it was stuck in traffic, and he came almost running to the airport.

In the meantime, at the airport, I was requesting the authorities to please wait since my husband was almost there.

Finally, Vikram reached, we got that girl's immigration done and almost ran to catch our Singapore Airlines flight to Singapore. The doors of the flight closed just after we stepped onto it. An experience which can never be forgotten in our lifetime.

There is one more incident which we can never forget. But this is a very beautiful experience. During our tours, we used to meet many people, and they used to observe the way we were taking care of the passengers who were travelling with us. Though our approach to our tourism profession was with a high level of professionalism, yet we maintained a warm, family-like atmosphere with our clients. This combination allowed us to provide exceptional service while fostering a sense of personal connection and hospitality.

It so happened that one lady who was travelling on our flight to Singapore approached me and later sent her mother, who was aged 78 years, with us on our Thailand, Malaysia, and Singapore tour. The old lady was very enthusiastic, but her age did not permit her to walk for a long time. In Bangkok, there is a park called Safari Park where you must walk a lot to see different shows. Here is where Vikram took the initiative to help that aunty in a wheelchair. She was a bit hesitant initially, but Vikram convinced her that if her own son had come along with her, he would have done the same thing. She then became comfortable. Vikram showed her the Safari World in Bangkok, the Dream World in Pattaya, and also the Jurong Bird Park in Singapore on a wheelchair.

It was the year 2004 when we both went to see the movie "Lakshya". Looking at the beauty of Ladakh and the bravery of our soldiers who fought in the Kargil war, in the theatre itself, Vikram and I decided that we must visit this place at least once. Immediately, Vikram started working on it and he asked his close friend Anuradha Prabhudesai if she could join us on this tour to Ladakh. She also agreed, and we four went to the beautiful heaven on earth, Ladakh. It was a very difficult terrain since oxygen is very low there. But the beauty was amazing. We were impressed by seeing it on the big screen, but to see and feel it with your own eyes was mesmerizing.

Our very first trip to Ladakh was an adventurous journey and hence the most memorable one. We took a flight to Delhi and onwards, we travelled to Manali on a night journey. It takes almost two days by road to travel to Leh from Manali. We were all prepared for this journey.

However, we came to know that the road was totally washed away due to heavy rains and landsliding. Now we were left with two options: either go to Delhi and fly back home, or since we had come up to Manali, go to visit the nearby places and enjoy Manali.

But Vikram was inspired by the movie "Lakshya" and the song kept lingering in his mind, "Lakshya ko haar haal me pana hai." And now his Lakshya (goal) was to anyhow reach Leh. Here, his friend Anuradha Prabhudessai supported him on this decision.

On enquiring with the tourist centre, they gave us a suggestion to drive to Chandigarh and fly to Leh. We immediately booked a cab, drove to Chandigarh on the same day, and took our flight to Leh the next day. It was indeed a very adventurous experience since it was raining heavily throughout our journey. But once we reached Leh, to our surprise, there was absolutely no rain anywhere, and it was totally dry.

Normally, people take rest for 24 hours to acclimatize to the low oxygen there. We were not aware of this, and we climbed the Shanti Stupa there on the very same evening. We met a man who randomly asked us when we had reached Leh. When he came to know that we had reached Leh on the same day and had climbed steps to reach the Shanti Stupa, he literally shouted at us and told us to immediately go to our hotel and take a rest, since this is low oxygen terrain. We may fall sick if we don't do that.

Today, when we take a group of people with us and ask them to rest for 24 hours to get acclimatized to the climate, we laugh at the adventure we had on our very first visit to Leh.

The movie 'Lakshya' was basically about the Kargil war. At that time, little did we know about this war which was fought in Drass and Kargil. Sitting in our cozy homes in Mumbai, we were not aware of how our enemy had cheated on us and how our motherland was in danger. Our brave heart soldiers had fought tooth and nail in this difficult terrain. One can understand the gravity of it when you see the height of Tiger Hill at Drass. This war was named "Operation Vijay."

The moment we saw the "Vijay Stumbh" at Drass, tears kept rolling down on seeing such young boys who had laid their lives for our motherland. This moment was an inspiration for us, and we took an oath there. We said we shall visit this place every year for the next five years, to bow down to these brave hearts.

that is till 2024, we have been celebrating Rakshabandhan festival at Ladakh and Kargil and shall continue until the time we can. We name this tour as "Mission Ladakh – Beauty with Bravery" since it's really a mission every year.

As per the oath that we had taken, immediately we took a group of twenty people the next year. I had joined this mission since I had missed the road route from Manali to Leh on our very first trip. During this journey, there is a place called Sarachu. A very beautiful plateau, but here is where we meet with the air which has very little oxygen. People really become "still" like a statue, and they are not able to lift the water bottle lying in front of them. It's a tough situation since the brain, which controls your actions, does not receive the necessary oxygen. There is tented accommodation here.

We reached this place in the late evening. Vikram's situation was no different. But being the tour leader, he was directing everyone to their respective tents. He was vomiting there, but without losing his confidence, he directed everyone, including me. After everyone had gone into their respective tents, he forgot in which tent I was. It was too cold and hence I had covered myself with the whole mattress from head to toe. So, in that state of health, he continued searching for me and finally found me inside the mattress. Today we laughed out loud at this episode, but during the episode, the situation was very panicky.

As we started this mission, we used to visit army regiments and tie Rakhis to the soldiers. When we used to tie rakhi on their wrists, the loving gesture in their eyes would fill our hearts with immense gratitude. Due to their job profile, they are not able to go to their homes for Raksha Bandhan. So, they are overwhelmed to see that there is a sister who is tying this Bandhan of love on their wrist. Some army personnel like Colonel Bakshi (name changed for security purposes) started knowing us and appreciated us for this unique mission.

In one of our tours to Ladakh, while returning from Kargil, there was a cloudburst and it started raining cats and dogs, and the connecting bridge from Khalse had collapsed. It was a very panicky situation. Many people were caught unaware by this sudden natural calamity, and Vikram had to safeguard not only himself but all the twenty-eight people with him, of which twenty-one were young girls. Darkness had set in and after some time, it would have been a very grave situation, since it would be totally dark, and you would not be able to see anything in front of you. Those were the days when there were no mobile phones and no network in the Ladakh region. An urgent spontaneous decision was required. He asked the police standing there if any military camp was nearby. The police told him that there was no military camp nearby, but there was a military policy post just 1 km ahead. Vikram asked him whether he would allow us to go till there, to which he agreed. Vikram went there, and from there he called Colonel Bakshi(name changed for security purposes), who was in LEH. The moment Vikram called him, he said, “I was waiting for your call. I knew you all must have been stranded somewhere but was just not aware where you got stuck. Now that you have told me where exactly you are, I shall send someone to pick your group."

What a relief it was! The Colonel himself had assured Vikram, and then our group was taken to the military regiment nearby. In our home, if suddenly we get even four guests, we get confused about how to be good hosts. Here was a group of twenty-eight people suddenly going to a military regiment to stay overnight. But a big, big hats off to our Bravehearts. They immediately prepared Sheera, puri, aloo sabzi, dal, rice, papad, and made the whole group comfortable. They brought mattresses from the nearby village, and before going to bed, they gave a bell button saying that in case you need anything, please press this and "banda" will come to your help. In the morning, the situation became better, and the group could slowly move ahead. But before leaving the regiment, they prepared poha for breakfast, tea, and biscuits. An experience which brings goosebumps whenever we try to recollect it. A big, big salute to our Indian Army.

There is one more small incident which could have been skipped easily, but since we were looking at everything in our Ladakh tour as a life experience, we could not let go of this. When we went to Nubra Valley, we saw a soldier standing with a gun in his hand near one of the military posts. On our return journey that was almost 24 hours after we had passed from that road, we saw the same soldier standing there. We stopped and asked him, "How many hours of duty do you people have?" He replied, "My buddy is sick, so I will stand here till he comes."

And he said this with a smiling face. Since Vikram was working in a bank, he immediately said that in our bank, if someone is absent for a day or two, his colleague is so frustrated because he has to manage two desks. And here was a soldier who was standing with a gun for 24 hours with a smiling face since his buddy was not well. We all learned a big lesson that day.

CHAPTER 6

Mission Ladakh

Our mission to Ladakh once a year has now become like an annual pilgrimage. In one of such missions in the year 2009, it so happened that there was sudden unrest in Srinagar. Usually, we would go from Kargil, via Zozila pass to Srinagar and fly back to Mumbai. But since Zozila pass was closed, we had to take a brave decision of going back by road all the way to Manali and Delhi and then fly back home. In this long journey back home, a bus dashed into our Scorpio and Vikram was injured. His ribs were damaged, and it was a very crucial time for us. One thing was good, it happened on the last day of the mission. In this incident, the mistake was that of the bus driver. We could have made a police complaint also. But this would have created unnecessary panic among our people and would have taken a long time to solve the issue. Here again Vikram took a brave decision and told me that we are going back to Mumbai. If we make any police complaint, all of us will have to wait here for 3 to 4 days to complete all the formalities and this would disturb the schedule of the people who had come with us, and we won't make any complaint and proceed. Here I remember the words of my Guru Mahatria, "Individual interest should be sacrificed for the larger interest"

We had to leave our vehicle there only. We used to travel with six people in one Scorpio. So now we had to adjust in other vehicles. Each one cooperated, and our journey back to Delhi began.

It was really a difficult situation for me, since I was seeing his pain, and this fellow was taking the decision to go back to Mumbai immediately. It took 3 days for us to reach Mumbai. Vikram was in too much pain. But he had tied a towel around his ribs till we reached Mumbai. We went to the doctor immediately, and the doctor advised him to complete rest and advised him to tie a rib band. The doctor was in shock to see how this man could travel for 3 days with this intense pain. Four of his ribs were fractured. Two days later, both our parents came, and we both got a big firing to stop this mission immediately. Vikram's mother convinced him very emotionally, and we were left with no option but to say "yes" to them until it was January 2010.

Now, again, Vikram started becoming restless, and he wanted to go to Ladakh. His injury had a big impact on his sugar levels. So, I was also worried and convinced him that we should stop this mission. But Vikram reminded me that in Drass, there is a war memorial in the name of Captain Manoj Pandey, and his words are engraved there which say, "IF DEATH STRIKES BEFORE I PROVE MY BLOOD, I SWEAR, I WILL KILL DEATH."

With this big inspiration in front of him, my convincing would make him weak. Hence, I supported him and again in

2010, we were in Ladakh with a group of people celebrating Raksha Bandhan with our soldiers. Seeing our determination to go to Ladakh every year, despite the tough situations we faced there, my mother got motivated, and she desired to come with us to this terrain. That year it so happened that just one week before we could leave, there was a cloud burst in Ladakh. There was water clogging everywhere. In the news, they were showing cars floating in the water. Again, a big question was there in front of us. But we decided to call our agent in Ladakh, Mr. Chosspell, and he assured us that if you bring your group, all arrangements will be done properly.

Out of the total group, ten people dropped out saying that they were scared to come with us. Here, a big salute to my mother, since she had complete faith in me, and Vikram and she came along with us on this year's mission. She had reached the age of 70, but she managed the whole mission quite easily and was very proud of her daughter and son-in-law. She was completely moved by Vikram's commitment. We heard this recent dialogue "ek bar maine commitment kar di to mai apnea ap ki bhi nahi sunta" from the movie Wanted But Vikram lived by this dialogue in that year's Mission Ladakh.

In one of our missions to Ladakh in 2017, one of our friends, Ms. Vinaya, had a friend named Pallavi. Pallavi's husband was a Group Captain in the Air Force and was posted in Leh. It was such a privilege to meet someone from the Air Force. That year we had seven young children in our group. The Group Captain motivated all the young children by telling them that in whatever profession they choose, they must excel. There must be utter sincerity in whatever they do in life.

We had invited them for dinner at our hotel. He made a very profound statement that time. He said that looking at all the youngsters, I feel once again Shivaji can be born. We are lacking a "Jijabai." The parents nowadays are pampering their children a lot and are not allowing them to be brave enough to handle the day-to-day difficulties in life.

So, by now, we had achieved good stability in our insurance and investment profession, our international tours, and Mission Ladakh. Vikram now came up with a very bold decision that he would quit his secure bank job and concentrate on these three aspects. He used to always say that he would not work for anyone after the age of 45, and correctly he was leaving his job at age 46. He took a voluntary exit from the bank. We were securing the financial boundaries of families from enemies like death, medical sickness, and helping them to grow their finances. Also, we were taking people to show the soldiers who were securing our boundaries from our enemies.

There was a big thought lingering in Vikram's mind, to start some organization through which we can create awareness about what our soldiers are doing for us standing at the borders. They have their families who are far away from them, especially the parents of soldiers. We see so many parents around us who pamper their children a lot. What guts these parents must have to send their child to the border where you never know what will happen. He shared this thought with his friend Anuradha Prabhudesai, who immediately agreed. And on 4th October 2009, Lakshy Foundation was formed with this pure intention of creating awareness among our young generation and invoking the soldier within them in whatever field of work they are.

CHAPTER 7

Million-Dollar Round Table Conference

In the journey of life, we had become quite stable in all roles. There was a transition from financial uncertainty to a place of stability and comfort. Since Vikram had fulfilled most of my dreams, my expectations of him naturally increased. We were now riding our blue beauty, our Kinetic Honda, and by now we had also upgraded from a two-wheeler to a four-wheeler. A grey WagonR had now become our family member. What a proud feeling it is to sit beside your husband in our own car and go for long drives. I remember the conversation we both had when we were going for a long drive in our car.

We were just two of us and the moment Vikram started the car, he smiled at me and said, "Aparna, can you believe it? After all the years of saving and planning, finally we are taking our own car for a long drive! Remember those nights when we'd sit and budget, cutting back on things just to save a little extra? It feels so good knowing we didn't give up." I immediately replied, "Yes, dear, this car is not just a vehicle for me. It's a symbol of everything that we've worked together, every bit of effort that we have put in, every sacrifice, it's all worth it now. And today sitting next to you in our own car, I say sorry for the sarcastic remark I had passed on you a few years back when you used to travel in Nitin's car." It was remarkable to see how far we had come. From uncertain beginnings to a life filled with abundance and adventure.

We travelled to various destinations like Europe, Singapore, Thailand, Malaysia, Hong Kong, and the most beautiful destination Ladakh in our own country. The Disneyland in Paris gave an absolute feeling like "Alice in Wonderland." The twin towers of Kuala Lumpur, the Sentosa Island in Singapore, and Burj Khalifa in Dubai are a few examples of how manmade creations can be so mesmerizing.

Also, we had done individual trips within our own country to Darjeeling, Nepal, Shimla, Manali, etc. The early morning sunrays on the Kanchenjunga ranges are a beauty which no words can express. Our joy soared beyond measure. The three of us had little interest in any materialistic possessions. I used to tell Vikram I am least interested in any jewellery or any rich clothing, but I wanted to explore the whole world. In all this, I really salute Vikram because he never made a big fuss about his diabetes. He would manage to take insulin twice a day. It was really a big challenge, but he was able to manage it.

Now, here again I started asking Vikram, we have seen many destinations, but how can we see the superpower country America? The scope of my dream had increased by now because

I had a partner in crime who was fulfilling all my dreams. He was the magician who made my dreams come true.

Since we are insurance agents, there is a target to be achieved, and with that, we would qualify for a degree called, "MILLION-DOLLAR ROUND TABLE CONFERENCE," the abbreviation of which is MDRT. So, as I have already mentioned, Vikram is a man of his words; he immediately took a VRS in 2010. He was now a free bird like me, and he started doing insurance business with full enthusiasm. We qualified for MDRT on 28th December 2010.

Our Development Officer, Mr. Bawkar, used to tell us that we could have qualified for MDRT way back in 2005. But some things can only be achieved when your heart feels it strongly and your mind conceives it. Insurance agents mostly try to qualify for MDRT as a prestige or an additional income. Here were Vikram and Aparna, who qualified for MDRT since they had a dream of going to the United States of America. We both literally danced that night since it was an additional feather in our cap.

Here again the tourist in us took over. We had some long discussions on this. This time I was the one who took the initiative. I asked Vikram, "Do you feel that here also, instead of only two of us going to the US for the conference, let's ask other agents if they would join us? After taking so many international tours, I am confident of doing a tour to this destination also." Vikram was a bit hesitant, but ultimately agreed and said, "Okay, if you have confidence, let's plan a proper tour along with our

MDRT meet." We started enquiring with other agents if they would be interested in joining this tour with us. To our surprise, thirty insurance agent friends showed interest in joining us at the conference.

But getting a US visa was the toughest part. And as we went for our visa, twenty people got their visas rejected, and now we were only ten people left to go to the conference. We were really feeling bad for those whose visas were rejected, but for all of us who had the stamped visa, we had a proud feeling. We remembered the dialogue in Deewar. "Mere pas US visa hai." However, Vikram was firm that we should take this first US tour even though we had only ten people with us. So, we made the necessary arrangements and went to the MDRT and did a tour of the east coast of the USA.

The MDRT meeting was in Atlanta in June 2011. We went to Atlanta on 24th June 2011. We had travelled to many destinations, but somehow landing in Atlanta was really something that gave us goosebumps. We travelled to Europe, which is only an 8-hour flight from Mumbai. This was double the distance and the most powerful country, something we had achieved to come here. It was such a grand welcome on the red carpet where they greeted you. Insurance agents from all over the world meet here and share their ideas. It was a mesmerizing experience.

From there, we went to Orlando, Niagara Falls, Washington, the White House, the great Times Square, and the Statue of Liberty. While standing in front of the White House, which is the residence of the President of the USA, we saw that there were no security guards anywhere. We asked our guide how come there were no security guards for such a prestigious place? The guide replied that there are hidden cameras here. In case anyone tries to do any mischief, they shall be caught within a fraction of a second. Here we realised what makes the USA a powerful country!

We came back with a lot of happiness and a proud feeling of attending the MDRT meeting in the USA.

By now, Rohan had grown up enough to know that his father was going to fulfil the dreams which we dream. So now he started telling Vikram, you both saw America, what about me? I also want to see the most powerful country. By now Vikram was a free bird to do business and he was confident that he had the capacity to fulfil our dreams.

So immediately the next year in 2012, we went to see the west coast of the USA. We saw the Golden Gate in San Francisco, Los Angeles, and Las Vegas. Since Vikram was himself an artist, he was very much interested in seeing HOLLYWOOD. So, we visited Universal Studios where they have a tour to show how the shooting of Hollywood movies is done. The three of us enjoyed this trip to the fullest.

After enjoying the USA for two consecutive years, it was time for an annual checkup for Vikram, which is mandatory for a diabetic person. But we had missed it in our hectic schedule of going to the USA. It was not only hectic physically, but also a lot of money was required to spend for two US tours. Hence, it was a very stressful period for Vikram.

So, we went for his routine checkup in the year 2012 and were shattered to see that Vikram's stress test had come back positive.

Immediately, we rushed to our doctor, Dr. Harshad Limaye. He advised that with a history of diabetes, an angiography had to be done and if they find any blockages, an immediate angioplasty would be required. The estimated cost of that would be around Rs. 2 lakhs. Now, we did not have this balance in our account. This issue could not be discussed with our family either. Now we had a big question in front of us. The test was mandatory, and we did not have enough money for the same. Most ladies do not want to sell off any of their ornaments unless it is too much of a crucial situation.

But now, this was a crucial situation indeed. So, I started working on some solutions. I had two bangles called "toda," which could easily fetch around Rs. 2.5 lakhs if sold. I suggested this option to Vikram. Initially, he was reluctant, but then I said this is the best option as of now. Let's see what happens later. Vikram assured me that he would make the same ornament for me as early as possible.

In the angiography, nothing much serious was found, and we absolutely had a sigh of relief.

The doctor only suggested being very careful and maintaining a healthy lifestyle. Within 3 years' time, Vikram made the same ornament for me. And the most important fact was that when we repeated a stress test after a gap of five years, it came back as negative. Vikram literally had tears in his eyes when he was reading this report and as a family we went through an immense feeling of pride and fulfilment. What a journey!

LION DOLLAR ROUND TABLE CONFE
ATLANTA, U.S.A.

CHAPTER 8

Subordinate Your Likes and Dislikes to the Purpose of Your Life

Now, again, we did not know what was coming in our life next. Our very good friend, Mr. Ramchandra Prabhudesai, told us that there is a session in Shanmukhanand Hall by Mr. T.T. Rangarajan, but somehow, we both could not attend this session. But little did we know that when the "student" within you is ready, a "teacher" comes into your life. Mr. Prabhudesai handed over some CDs by T.T. Rangarajan to us.

The journey began with a simple curiosity – a desire to explore new ideas and perspectives. Little did we know that this CD would become a catalyst for our personal growth and transformation. We watched the CD "dinacharya" and we felt like watching more and more of such CDs. So, we bought some CDs and kept watching. This was the time when our Life Guru, our beloved Mahatria, came into our life and from here onwards, he just carried us through.

So now we have been introduced to this path of Infinitheism. There was a programme called Infini Alpha and Mr. Vinod from Infinitheism came to meet us. The cost of the programme was Rs.30,000/- per person. Now again a big dilemma, whether to spend only Rs.30,000/- or Rs.60,000/- for both of us was really a big question. We told Vinod that we shall confirm in a day or two. But then Vinod convinced us how it was important that we both attend this programme and now we feel that cosmic energy only wanted both of us to be with him and that's the reason we both enrolled, and our new journey of life started.

We used to watch different videos on YouTube of Infinitheism. Till then, Vikram had a craving for non-veg food, but the same was not allowed at home, so he used to eat only non-veg food when we used to go for hoteling or with friends. As a big contrast, I am a pure vegetarian and don't eat even an egg. We, therefore, had to go to two different restaurants. First, Vikram used to eat non-veg in a restaurant, where I used to simply sit, and then we would go to a vegetarian restaurant, and I would relish my food. But we never stopped hoteling.

One day, suddenly to my utmost surprise, Vikram came and told me, rather promised me that he would never ever eat non-veg food henceforth. He had left it from that moment itself. Knowing Vikram very well, by now, I knew that what Vikram decides he decides. My happiness knew no bounds, but still, for curiosity's sake, I asked him, "Can you please explain to me what exactly happened? How come you have suddenly come to this conclusion?"

He shared with me that he had heard something very profound from Mahatria's video. He said, "Aparna, today I happened to see an old video of our dear Mahatria. In that video, Mahatria explained that when you shave and the blade scratches your cheek, causing you to bleed a little, is it a pleasurable experience? It hurts a lot, right! Then, when animals are killed to satiate the taste of your tongue for a few seconds, is it worth causing so much pain to someone?"

These words had really hit him so hard, and his heart literally cried out. He took an instant decision there and then that he wouldn't hurt any animal for his own taste. Of course, this is a very personal decision, but he kept his promise from that moment till today. At the same time, he totally stopped his occasional drinking also.

Here I would quote my Guru Mahatia: "There are two options in life: Either subordinate your likes and dislikes to the purpose of your life or subordinate the purpose of your life to your likes and dislikes." Obviously, Vikram decided to subordinate his likes and dislikes to the purpose of his life, which was to maintain his health. He was nearing his Half Century Birthday on 14th August 2014, so he became more conscious about healthy eating and a healthy lifestyle.

CHAPTER 9

Golden Milestone – Qualifying CFP At 50

In the dynamic world of finance, diversification and expansion are critical strategies for growth and stability. We were totally focused on the insurance business. But this versatile person, Vikram, recognized the potential benefits of branching out into the mutual fund sector. All eggs can't be kept in one basket for our clients. Here, since I had a fourteen-year experience of working with UTI, which was the first mutual fund of India, I initiated and cleared the AMFI exam, which is required to take up any mutual fund agency.

Insurance and mutual funds complement each other well. Insurance products provide financial protection against unforeseen events, while mutual funds offer investment opportunities for wealth accumulation. This synergy allows us to present a more holistic financial planning service to our clients.

Now Vikram started realizing that mutual funds were the future of the finance industry. Also, people in metros like

Mumbai were more interested in investing in mutual funds. To achieve a comprehensive understanding of such financial planning, Vikram decided to pursue a proper certified course known as "CFP" (Certified Financial Planner). This is a US-based course, and it requires a lot of study. Through some references, he got a teacher, Mr. Kulkarni, who used to teach these subjects of CFP. Many young people were enrolled there, and Vikram was the oldest at age 50. But once you decide something, then the world conspires to achieve it. Mr. Vinay Jadav, a very young boy, got friendly with Vikram, and he used to come over to our home, and they both used to study. They would study mostly in the evening since our full day would go in office work.

It was quite an experience. I would enter the bedroom at night and instead of finding a sleeping Vikram, he would be at his desk, with his spectacles on studying as if he were a young student giving exams. I would smile and ask him, "Coffee?" Now, I was not the only one watching this new Vikram, in a new role – but Rohan was too. He would watch his father study (often harder than him!) and slowly started absorbing his sincerity. So beautifully my Guru Mahatria says, why should your children investigate the outer world for some Role Models? They should look at their own parents for Role Models, and yes, Vikram has become a Role Model for Rohan for his sincerity and hard work.

These exams are to be given online and each paper was tough. Studying after a gap of 25 years, also taking an exam online and the subject, everything was really a stressful experience. But Vikram never gave up and was persistent on doing CFP, and finally he completed CFP. Our joy was boundless, and the same was the happiness with his teacher Mr. Kulkarni and his dear friend Vinay. His teacher was happier because Vikram used to declare the date when he would give the exam, appear on the same day, and clear the subject.

There is a complex interplay between a person's emotional and physical health. By now, we had clearly understood the relationship between Vikram's stress and his sugar levels. During all this process, his sugar levels fluctuated a lot, and hence he was advised insulin before every meal, that is thrice a day.

It was a thing of concern for us, but one thing was very good that doctors were happy that except sugar levels, all other parameters were totally fine, and this rarely happens with diabetic people. His doctor Dr.Abjijeet Jadhav smiles and says, Vikram just knows to manage his diabetes well under all situations and also with increasing age.

We are proud of our armed forces who gave their "TODAY" for our better "TOMORROW". As civilians, we hoist and unfurl our national flag on 15th August and 26th January every year. But to see someone ready to give his life for the same was very inspiring.

Vikram also got so much inspired by the dedication of the soldiers, seeing their fitness, that he started making some changes in his diet and decided that he should do some exercise daily. He started realising that there must be great discipline in our day-to-day life.

Now again, Vikram was a person who always had something unique in his mind. He asked me, "Aparna, I have one thought in my mind. Why should we come alone every year? Let us try to bring along some friends or relatives with us to show them this beauty plus bravery of Ladakh and Kargil. What is your opinion on this?" For a minute, I was stunned by this question. We were hardly settling in taking international tours, but bringing people to this terrain seemed very challenging. But still, I replied, "My dear, I have now complete faith in your thoughts and your thoughts manifest into things which I have witnessed. So, I agree with your new innovative idea."

Now that it was decided to bring along more people with us to Ladakh, this man came up with another idea. He again asked me, "Aparna, how about celebrating Rakshabandhan festival with our soldiers? It would be such a nice gesture to tie rakhi on the wrist of these brave hearts who are protecting us from our enemies, while we are peacefully sleeping in our cosy homes, isn't it?" I immediately agreed to this. From that year till today,

CHAPTER 10

Your Life is Your Responsibility

Conflict between two generations is a timeless theme. A time comes in the life of every father and grown-up son that they have controversies in every aspect of life. The son is growing up into a man, and the father is still the grown-up man who feels he should guide his son properly in all aspects of life. This strained relationship leads to frequent arguments and a growing emotional distance between them. The mother is the victim of this situation because she has a husband on one side and a son on the other.

This typical situation started developing in our house, and again I did not want Vikram to get stressed. This situation was so fragile that we could not discuss it with our own parents. The three of us were living as a nuclear family.

Recognising the deepening rift, I thought of seeking help from our Guru Deipakk bhai. I called him and narrated the situation to him. To my surprise, he asked both of us to meet him and said there was no need to bring Rohan along. He again surprised us by telling us there is never an issue with the child. The parents need to correct themselves. He told Vikram that now it's time for "you" to change. Your ways of saying should be different. You are now dealing with a young adult. Vikram kept these words in his mind. But implementation of this was difficult.

While listening to one of the speeches of our Life Guru Mahatria, Vikram had a profound realisation. The experiences which life gives you teach you many things. So, the day Rohan turned 21, he told Rohan, "From now on, your life is your responsibility. For any type of help you need, we are always there for you, but from now onwards, no advice from my side." Vikram has kept this promise till date, and that has really made Rohan grow into a very good person. He completed his mechanical engineering with distinction, did his master's in industrial engineering at the University of Texas at Arlington - USA and is now currently working in LOS ANGELES. Not only in the materialistic aspect, but he has grown into a very humble human being.

Finding the right home is always a challenging task, especially when the family has outgrown the current space. For us, this realization hit hard when our son,

Rohan visited India in 2019 and told us that it's time we shift to a bigger house. We were living in a one BHK home of 410 sq feet and we both were also feeling the need for a bigger home but could not dare to practically do it. But now here was our young son who was telling us to take this step and that he was there to support us in all aspects, including finance.

The decision to move was inevitable, but where to move was the central question. After all, a house is more than just walls and a roof; it's where memories are made and where your heart truly resides.

Life had swapped roles. Our son Rohan, though he right now lives in Los Angeles, had spent his whole life in Vile Parle East only. So, he was a bit adamant that if we were to move, it had to be within the same neighborhood. His insistence wasn't just a matter of convenience or familiarity; it was about the deep connection he felt to the area, Vile Parle East, with its tree-lined streets, close-knit community, and the typical Maharashtrian culture. For him, it was more than just a place on the map. For him, it was a home. Vikram's feelings were no different than Rohan.

So, with a big daring, we started looking for a good home in Vile Parle. By now, we had that strong faith in our minds that our dear Mahatria is there with us, and he will carry us through.

It was a very big decision indeed. But to our surprise, we saw a terrace flat in Vile Parle of 832 sq. feet, and we all were really lured to buy this flat. But it was going beyond our budget. Here, now I want to specially thank my sister and her husband, Dr. Ashwini and Dr. Uday Joglekar, my Kaku Mrunal Joshi, and my brother-in-law and sister-in-law, Mr. Vivek and Mrs. Swati Joshi.

They all told us that at this point they could raise some funds for us and literally they gave us Rs. 10 lakhs each, which of course we returned as early as possible. But Vikram and I literally had happy tears in our eyes. We are surrounded by such a blessed family. What more can we ask from God?

We only have gratitude to be blessed. Also, we had to arrange for a loan of Rs. 1 crore ten lakhs. I am specifically mentioning the amount because Vikram was nearing his 60s, and we had taken such risks.

However, we nullified the loan by the end of 2023. A small regret that both our parents and my uncle could not see this new home in person, since we lost all of them in the years 2015 to 2017. But still, we feel their presence since all this would not be possible without their blessings. Physically, they are not with us, but emotionally we never miss them.

CHAPTER 11

Be A 60-Year-Old Whom All Other 60-Year-Olds Would Look Up To

Life has a curious way of teaching us lessons when we least expect them. Sometimes, these lessons come in the form of unexpected losses, and other times they emerge from our determination to keep a promise, no matter the cost. My experience in 2019 with Jet Airways and Sri Lankan Airways taught me that even in the face of financial loss, the value of commitment and honoring one's word can create a memorable journey.

The incident goes like this...

I had meticulously planned our regular tour to Singapore with a total of forty passengers. During those days, JET AIRWAYS was the airline of my choice, a company I had used multiple times in the past without incident, and all our tickets were booked on the same. However, fate had other plans.

We were just 5 days away from our departure and suddenly I was blindsided by the news that JET AIRWAYS had suspended all their flights and declared themselves bankrupt, announcing that they would not fly any flights until further notice. Panic set in as I realised that the money invested in those tickets might never be recovered. But again, Vikram being Vikram, he said that once committed, always committed. He said that he wasn't going to let the setback with JET airways deter us from our promise to take this tour.

We immediately started looking for options, and we booked on Sri Lankan Airlines via Colombo – Singapore. We had to shell out Rs.6 lakhs from our pocket to book those tickets. Cancelling the tour was not an option since all our hotel bookings in Singapore were done. Also, Jet Airways promised that they would refund our money, but to date, our money is still with them. We have not received that money back.

Since we had to shell out so much money at one time, we were left with a very minimal balance in our account. We shall remain ever grateful to our staff,

Mr. Jitu Patel, Mr. Nilesh Patel, Mrs. Kavita Matvankar, and my maid Smt. Sevanti Pradhan, because they agreed to take half the salary for 2 months. Of course, we gave them the balance once the financial position improved, but it was really a great gesture from their end to understand our position and support us at the time of need. All of them have been working with us for the last 20 years.

At the end of the same year in December 2019, one of my friends, Varsha, suggested that we should explore the Northeast sector. As we are basically travelers, we immediately agreed to it, and I also asked one of my other friends, Kalpana, if she would be interested in joining us. By now, in our friend circle, everyone knew that if Vikram or Aparna are planning some tour, it will be a well-organized tour. So, she also immediately agreed to join.

We seven of us went on an eighteen-day tour to the most beautiful place in our country, Assam, Meghalaya, Arunachal, in February 2020. Nestled in the northeastern part of India, these states boast a stunning array of landscapes, from snow-capped mountains and lush green valleys to pristine rivers and dense forests. We also visited the cleanest village in Asia, Mawlynnong. It is renowned for its cleanliness and eco-friendly practices.

Our annual Mission of Ladakh was due on 10th August 2019. On 5th August, our government abolished ACT 370. Now, this again was such a fragile situation; would there be any unrest in the Kargil area? But as we have complete faith in our agents of Ladakh and Kargil, we called our Sadik bhai in Kargil about what the situation was, to which he replied, "yaha sab albel hai, you can come here without any tension."

We took our group to Drass Kargil, like every year. Sadik bhai was overwhelmed to see us there. Many groups had cancelled their tours to Kargil because of the fear. But Vikram and I were there with our group, and we had an excellent mission like every year.

Our beloved Guru Mahatria had taught us, "Doubt until you develop trust. Once trusted, never doubt again." Hence, we could achieve the Kargil sector in 2019 because of our faith in our Sadik bhai in Kargil.

The year 2020 came as a big bang in everyone's life all over the world. We were totally unaware of the pandemic which had just started cropping up. We enjoyed our tour to the fullest and came back and were now preparing to move to our new home. The date on which we moved to our new home is really a historic date which we can never forget, 21st March 2020. The next day, a lockdown was announced, and we were in this empty flat until the pandemic was over.

We had sold our office and had moved to an office on rent. But because of this pandemic, we had to keep paying the rent for three years but could not utilize it. However, our work did not stop since our clients had to pay their premiums on time and mutual fund SIPs had to continue for our clients. A big learning from this pandemic was that we could sit in our home and still run our office work. Even people who were not so tech-savvy could pay their premiums online. Hence, in 2023, we discontinued our office and provided computers to my staff in their homes.

So now, everyone is happy, peaceful, and our work is still going on smoothly.

One thing I would mention here is that we paid the full salary of our staff and our maid during the whole pandemic period.

During the pandemic period, Vikram's health was the main concern. But happy to share that he sailed through the pandemic totally hale and hearty. He had joined an online Zumba class, and his routine of taking care of his health continued.

As our beloved Guru Mahatria keeps telling us that the body that we are gifted is a temple. Just like how we keep sacredness in the temple, our body should also be kept well-maintained and totally fit. Give your body one hour of exercise, and it will take care of you for the rest of 23 hours. These words hit Vikram so strongly, and from here onwards, Vikram started taking more care of his health. He now regularly goes to the gym. His trainer is very happy to see his sincerity for his health. Now, he tries to adjust all his daily routines without missing his gym.

Despite taking so much care, his sugar levels were okay, but after every 15 days, he used to get a severe cold and had to take antibiotics for this. Here, our dear son Rohan once told him to take a cold-water shower daily. Life had swapped roles. The father had to obey some things told by his son. So, Vikram now started taking cold water showers and to our utter surprise, his cold has totally vanished. He is a person who takes cold water showers in Ladakh also and has saved himself from frequent attacks of cold.

It is such a proud feeling that his doctor, Dr. Abhijeet Jadhav, said that Vikram knows how to control his diabetes. He once said that we, as doctors, tell all our patients how to keep their diabetes under control. You are a role model patient. You should be an inspiration to them.

Our Mission Ladakh 2024 was scheduled for 1st August 2024. It was the birthday month of Vikram, and he was to complete his age 60 on 14th August 2024. We had a group of thirty people. On the very first day of the tour, we had to take five of them to a hospital in Leh since they were experiencing all the symptoms of nausea and vomiting. Vikram and I took care of them until late at night but brought them hale and hearty back to the hotel. This year's mission was full of illness. We had to visit all hospitals including Kargil, Nubra Valley, and Pangong Lake. The average age of people who were getting ill was ranging between 30 to 45. Here was the 60-year-old Vikram who was helping them to go to the hospital and bringing them back fit to resume the mission. Anyways, this is also an experience to be learned.

Especially when in Ladakh, what I feel is: Vikram is so much devoted and so much in love for our armed forces that, along with God, all the army men take care of his health and in turn he takes care of others' health in Ladakh.

His devotion towards this work just carries him through.

Seeing our dedication to this mission, one of Vikram's friends, Raju Wagh, who is an expert in making handmade frames in Origami, made four beautiful frames and handed them over to us on the previous day of our departure. This was his love for the soldiers. When we handed over these beautiful frames to the officers in the Air Force and to a Major in the Army, they were overwhelmed to receive this beautiful gift. Mr. and Mrs. Punekar, a couple aged 80 and 75, live in our adjacent building. Last year, Mrs. Punekar was a witness to our function during Diwali when we lit the Akhand lamp for the long life of our soldiers. She was so moved by this that this year she herself made 1.5 kg besan ladoo and handed it over to us to give this sweet to our jawans. It was a very touching moment for me and Vikram.

This year we received a very touching message from one of the soldiers to whom I had tied the rakhi. It goes this way:

"Tai, tumhi bhetla, ani premane avarjun rakhi bandli, khup bhari vatla. Dolyatun pani nahi ala pan maan bharun ala hota. Bolayla Shabda navhte, karan khup kami loka bhettat amhala ashi. Itkaya dur asun tumhi nashibane bhetalat, prem ani apulki dakhavli, gharchya mansa pramane sakhya bahini pramane vaglat. Bhari vatla kharach, Thank you sooo much. Mumbai la alyvar nakki bhetu."

Translation: Dear Sister, you have come so far to tie rakhi to us is so overwhelming. I have not got tears in my eyes, but my heart is filled with gratitude. I don't have words to express my feelings. It was my good fortune that I met you, and I felt like I have met my real sister. Whenever I come to Mumbai, I shall surely meet you.

Such beautiful and touching messages give us inspiration to go to Ladakh again and again.

This year again, we were overwhelmed to meet the great personalities in the Air Force. They also admired our gesture of tying Rakhis to all of them.

This is Vikram's life journey which I have witnessed and have a proud feeling that I am his life partner. To put it in our Mahatria's words, "In a world that never believes anything unless they 'see' it, here was Vikram, whose rationale was, 'What you 'believe' in you will 'see'."

Rain fills the size of your vessel. Whether your life will be filled with abundance, scarcity, or adequacy depends on the size of your thinking. Thoughts manifest into things.

So, till now, we have always had abundance in our thoughts, and life has filled only with abundance.I conclude this book with a feeling of happiness, pride, aspirations, optimism and much love for Vikram, for Life and our family, friends and mentors – without whom none of what we are experiencing would have been possible.

Knowing Vikram, all I can say at the end is – I know it is just a beginning... who knows what next, what more will come into our lives!

I am ready.

SOME TESTIMONIALS FROM OUR FRIENDS AND RELATIVES:

DR. Bhooma Vashi

Orthodontist

The Braces Point - Andheri (West)

VIKRAM JOSHI with my perspective is.

V – Victorious

I – Inspiring

K – Kind

R – Remarkable

A – Aspiring

M – Modest

J – Joyful

O – Optimistic

S – Strong

H – Hard Working

I – Incredible

Vikram is indeed an inspiring personality. I met him along with his wife, Aparna, in our Guru Mahatria's spiritual programme called "Infini Alpha" long ago, and our friendship just clicked. We had an instant connection with each other. He has been like a passionate civilian who has deep devotion and patriotism for his country in his heart.

I encountered him when I went with my husband Dr. Nikhil on the Ladakh trip with Vikram and Aparna. A man of few words, completely committed to his roles, Vikram Joshi is.

When I experienced him on top of that mountain in Ladakh, talking about war zones, about how the warriors, our soldiers protect our country to keep all of us safe, I had a feeling that indeed he is carrying the energy of a soldier. His noble intention, his passion and mission for Lakshya Foundation, and his consistent efforts to take civilians to Leh Ladakh, Vijay Stumbh at Kargil, war memorial, etc., to create awareness in civilians about the hardships of army personnel and sensitising them to the facts of their lives is incredible.

He is helping civilians to be more responsible, patriotic, and truly grateful through these experiences in Ladakh, and they are indeed outstanding efforts. The thought of tying Raksha (rakhi) to the soldiers on or near the day of Raksha Bandhan by civilians is so beautiful. The act of tying rakhi to soldiers who are keeping our tricolour flying high and are ready to give their lives to keep us safe, standing tall in adverse weather conditions, with a heart full of emotions and prayers for their well-being in the war zone, has left a deep impact on my heart.

He is an amazing poet and an artist. Listening to his poetry on our Bravehearts brought tears to my eyes.

Vikram has taught by example that by living with discipline, one can manage a disease like insulin-dependent diabetes. How the lifestyle changes and consistent self-motivated intelligent efforts can keep him fit that he has shown through his actions.

I am sure that the story of his life, in the form of this book, which is a beautiful idea by his loving wife Aparna, will inspire many people to manage diabetes and stay fit in life. I wish the best for this book.

VIVEK JOSHI (Vikram's elder brother)

Retired from IDBI Bank.

And Stage artist

विक्रम...६० वर्षांचा झाला...पण त्याच्याकडे पाहून असं अजिबातच वाटत नाही.... मी जरी त्याचा मोठा भाऊ असलो तरी त्याच्या वागण्याबोलण्यामुळे तोच मोठा असावा असाही अनेकांचा समज होतो...

त्याच्याविषयी सांगायची सुरवात करताना पूर्ण साठ वर्षं मागे जावं लागेल...माझ्या जन्मानंतर माझ्या आजीने मी तिचा पहिलाच नातू असल्यामुळे मला अत्यंत कौतुकाने सांभाळलं पण अडीच वर्षांनंतर विक्रमचा जन्म झाल्यावर यापुढे मी दोघांनाही सांभाळणार नाही हे तिने जाहीर करून टाकल्यामुळे सहाव्या महिन्यातच विक्रमची रवानगी माझ्यासह पाळणाघरात झाली...काही माणसांच्या बाबतीत असं होतं की त्यांची काहीही चूक नसताना, त्यांनी काहीही केलेलं नसताना त्यांना विनाकारण एखाद्या गोष्टीसाठी शिक्षा भोगावी लागते..विक्रमच्या बाबतीत हा सिलसिला जो त्याच्या वयाच्या सहाव्या महिन्यापासून सुरू झाला तो आजतागायत सुरूच आहे...

आईबाबा दोघंही नोकरी करत असल्यामुळे सहाव्या महिन्यापासूनच त्याला पाळणाघरात ठेवलं...त्यामुळे त्याची तब्येत इतकी बिघडली की त्याला hospital मधे admit करावे लागले....पुढे काही दिवसातच असं लक्षात आलं की तो डावखुरा आहे... त्याकाळी डावखुरा असणं योग्य नव्हे अशी बहुतांशी धारणा असल्यामुळे त्याला उजवा करण्याचे प्रयत्न सुरू झाले...ते त्याच्यावर इतकं लादलं गेलं की तो अर्धा उजवा आणि अर्धा डावरा झाला...एकदा मी मागून कुत्र्याची शेपटी ओढली आणि पुढच्या बाजूला उभ्या असलेल्या विक्रमला कुत्रा चावला... मी अभ्यास न करता उनाडक्या केल्या म्हणून माझ्या बरोबर त्याच्यावरही उगाचंच घरून बंधनं आली...college मधे एका मुलाचा खून झाला तेंव्हा त्या मुलाशी काही वर्षांपूर्वी विक्रमचं भांडण झालं होतं हे कारण सांगून चौकशीसाठी पोलीसांनी दिवसभर त्याला पोलीस station मधे बसवून ठेवलं होतं, वयाच्या २९व्या

वर्षी काहीही संबंध नसताना अचानकच त्याला diabetes detect झाला... तो सुद्धा इतका severe की तो संपूर्णपणे insulin-dependent झाला...ही त्याचीच काही उदाहरणं..अशी आणखीही देता येतील...

पण अशावेळीही निराश होऊन, परिस्थितीला शरण जाऊन हातपाय गाळून बसलेलं मी त्याला कधीही बघितलेलं नाही...विपरीत परिस्थितित कसं वागलं पाहिजे, संकटांना धैर्याने कसं सामोरं जायला हवं ते त्याच्याकडून शिकण्यासारखं आहे....अभ्यासात तो कधीही मागे पडला नाही..M com, LLB केलंय त्याने...तो carrom उत्तम खेळतो, college चा champion होता तो...नाटकात उत्तम काम करायचा... अनेक बक्षिसं मिळवली आहेत त्याने त्यात...खरं सांगायचं तर उत्तम व्यक्तिमत्व, उत्तम आवाज, आणि अभिनयाची उपजत असलेली जाण...या गुणांमुळे तो या क्षेत्रात नक्कीच पुढे आला असता पण diabetes मुळे त्याच्यावर मर्यादा आल्या, या क्षेत्रातला अनियमितपणा, धावपळ तब्येतीसाठी घातक ठरू शकेल हे लक्षात घेउन आपल्या अत्यंत आवडत्या क्षेत्रातून तो स्वत:हून बाहेर पडला...ही खरं तर खूप कठीण गोष्ट आहे पण त्याने ती स्विकारली...आजही तो नाटक, मराठी, हिंदी, English सिनेमे आवर्जुन,आवडीने बघतो...त्याचा महत्वाचा गुण म्हणजे कुणाच्याही मदतीला तो वेळकाळ न बघता धावून जातो... आम्हा सर्व भावंडांशी त्यांचे अत्यंत प्रेमाचे,जिव्हाळ्याचे संबंध आहेत... आधी आसावरी मग रोहन आणि आता राधा हे तर त्याचे विशेष हळवे कोपरे आहेत...चांगलं जगायचं असेल तर आयुष्यात शिस्त, नियमितपणा महत्वाचा हे तत्व अंगिकारुन विक्रमची वाटचाल सुरू आहे, तो दृढनिश्चयी असल्यामुळे जे तो ते तो करून दाखवतो हे तर मी त्याच्याबाबतीत कायमच अनुभवत आलोय...

विक्रमविषयी सांगायचं तर अपर्णाचा उल्लेख अपरिहार्य ठरतो...कारण ती त्याच्या आयुष्यात आल्यावर त्याची झालेली प्रगती विशेष उल्लेखनीय ठरते...ही दोघंही चांगल्या नोक-या सोडून स्वत:च्या व्यवसायात यशस्वी झालेली "मराठी" माणसं आहेत...दोघांनाही पर्यटनाची प्रचंड आवड आहे... त्यांचे भारतासह इतरही अनेक देश बघून झालेत...

आता वयाच्या या विशिष्ट टप्प्यावर आल्यावरही मागे वळून न बघता विक्रमची शिस्तबद्ध वाटचाल अशीच पुढे अव्याहत चालू रहावी आणि त्याला जे जे करायचंय ते ते करण्यात त्याला यश मिळावं यासाठी माझ्याकडून त्याला खूप खूप शुभेच्छा...

(TRANSLATION)

Vikram has just reached age 60, but looking at him, no one can believe this. Though I am his elder brother, because of his overall behaviour, many people feel like he is the elder brother.

If I have to say anything about him, I will have to take my memory 60 years back. Me being the first grandson in the family, my grandmother happily took care of me. But when Vikram was born after 2.5 years, she declared that she couldn't take care of two children at a time and hence my parents had to keep little Vikram with a babysitter when he was just 6 months old. Both our parents were working.

It happens with some people that without any fault of theirs they must face many difficult situations, and Vikram, my younger brother, is one amongst them. In his case, it started from the age of 6 months and continues till today.

He was too small to be in a crèche, and he fell so sick that he had to be admitted to the hospital. After a few years, it was realised that he was a left-handed boy. Those were the days when if a person was left-handed, it was not considered a good thing. So now everyone started working on making him a right-handed boy, and in this process, he manages some things by the right hand and some by the left. In our teenage years, once I pulled the tail of a dog, but the dog bit Vikram who was standing close to the dog. Since I did not concentrate much on studies and did many other activities, Vikram had to face many restrictions from our parents. Once during his college days, he was detained at the police station by the police because one boy was murdered, and Vikram had a fight with that boy a few years back. At the very young age of 28, he was diagnosed with a disease like diabetes, and he must take insulin for a lifetime.

These are a few incidents where life threw many challenges at Vikram for no fault of his. There are many more incidents but can't share them all. But he has faced all challenges very bravely. He never went into depression, nor did he surrender himself to the situation.

One should learn from Vikram how to face the adversities of life, calmly and confidently. He was also brilliant in studies. He completed his M. Com and BGL. He is also good at playing carrom and has won many prizes. He was the carrom champion in his college. He is also a good actor and has won many prizes in interbank drama competitions. His personality, his voice modulation, his liking for acting were perfect to be a professional actor, but his insulin-dependent diabetes would not allow him to do all this for a long time. The schedules in this profession are very uncertain. All this would have hampered his health and so he volunteered to keep away from this acting field. Giving up your likings and staying away from them is not so easy, but still, he managed it for his health. But today also he watches good English, Hindi movies, and Marathi dramas.

Vikram is a person who is always the first person to help anyone, be it a relative or a friend. He has a very good relationship with all our relatives. My daughter Asavari and his son Rohan, and now our granddaughter Radha, are his weak points.

How to live a disciplined life is what one should learn from him. He always completes his commitments. Now when I speak so much about Vikram, Aparna's name is inevitable. After she came into his life, they both managed to reach many heights in life. Both left their jobs very early in life, and I have witnessed this Maharashtrian couple do business, rather a profession like finance consultant. Also, with their tourism profession, they have seen almost half the world.

Looking back at all this, I wish Vikram a very happy and disciplined life post 60...

PRACHI KANDALKAR

CLIENT AND FRIEND

RETIRED AS A.O. FROM BRIHANMUMBAI MUNICIPAL CORPORATION

आदरणीय विक्रम,

तुला हिरकमहोत्सवी वाढदिवसाच्या खूप साऱ्या शुभेच्छा 💐💐

मी तुला इथे आदरणीय म्हटलंय कारण खरंच तुझी जीवनशैली ही माझ्यासारख्या मधुमेहीं करीता नेहमीच आदर्श ठरलीय. वयाच्या 28 व्या वर्षी मधुमेह जडल्यानंतर कोणीही हादरले असते पण तू आपल्या शिस्तबद्ध स्वभावाने त्याला योग्य रीतीने धोपवून धरलेस. हे सर्व करताना तू आपले छंद जोपलेस,सामाजिक बांधिलकी जपलीस. चाकोरीबद्ध 10 ते 5 ह्या बँकेच्या नोकरीत जखडून राहिला नाहीस. गुंतवणूक सल्लागार म्हणून स्वतःला गुंतवलेस पण त्याचा अभ्यास ही केलास. ह्या क्षेत्रात स्वतःला update ठेवण्याकरिता नवनवीन जागतिक दर्जाचे कोर्स केलेस त्यामुळे आमच्यासारखे गुंतवणूकदार तुझ्याकडे डोळे झाकून निर्धास्तपणे आपली गुंतवणूक करू शकले. लेह लडाख ची tour आयुष्यात एकदा करताना मी तरी कित्येकदा कचरत होते पण तू दरवर्षी तिथे जाऊन लक्ष्य फॉउंडेशन चे कार्य करीत आहेस.तुझी रोजची दिनचर्या आखीव आहे.

हे सर्व करताना अर्थातच तुला अपर्णाची साथ आहेच. त्याशिवाय हे शक्य नाही. आयुष्यातील प्रत्येक प्रसंगाकडे सकारात्मक दृष्टीने पाहणे हा तुमचा दोघांचाही गुण आहे, आणि तोच प्रेरणादायी आहे.

अपर्णा, माझी तुला एक विनंती आहे की अशा ह्या बहुआयामी व्यक्तिमत्व असलेल्या विक्रम चे पार्ल्याच्या लोकमान्य संघात 'मजेस्टिक गप्पा 'मध्ये तू व्याख्यान आयोजित कर.

तर, विक्रम तुझे साठीनंतरचे आयुष्य हे असेच आनंदी, निरोगी जाऊ दे हीच सदिच्छा.

तुझी स्नेहांकित,

श्रीम. प्राची कांदळकर,

निवृत्त प्रशासकीय अधिकारी,

बृहन्मुंबई महागरपालिका

(TRANSLATION)

Respected Vikram

Wishing you a very happy diamond jubilee birthday. Here, I have addressed you as "respected", since you really are a role model for many diabetes people like me. If this disease struck anyone at the very young age of 28, any person would have gone into a very depressive state. But, with your disciplinary nature, you have controlled it very well. And at the same time, you have also done all the things for which you were so passionate. You have managed to do your hobbies also, and you are fulfilling your social obligations too. You did not stick to a typical 10 to 5 banking job. You quit your job at a very right age and became a finance consultant. In this profession also, you kept updating yourself by doing various courses in the finance field. Hence people like us can hand over our finance management to you with great trust. I was getting so scared to go to Leh Ladakh only once. But you keep going there every year, which is creditable. You have disciplined your daily routine. You have kept diseases like diabetes under control with your proper diet and exercise. I have experienced how you control your sweet tooth.

Of course, Aparna has a big role to play in your life. She is a perfect life partner. In whatever situation you both may face, you always have a very positive approach to it, and this is really a very inspirational thing.

Aparna, I have one request. Please arrange one lecture of Vikram in Vile Parle Majestic Gappa.

Vikram, I wish you a very healthy and happy life post 60 years.

SHASHANK BAWKAR

DEVELOPMENT OFFICER

LIC OF INDIA

It's been a matter of great pride and privilege to have Vikram Joshi as one of my close friends and a source of inspiration.

One thing I prominently observed about Vikram Joshi is that in spite of coming from a middle-class background with a salaried source of income, he not only dared to dream about travelling the globe, a dream which is far beyond the horizon of most of the people who come from his background, but he dreamt, planned, saved, and executed his dream into reality and travelled Europe and a lot of foreign countries which most of the people wished they could.

One more inspiring thing about Vikram is that even after learning about his insulin-dependent diabetic condition, which would have led an average person into the circle of worry and anxiety, instead of slowing down and taking it easy, he chose to deal with it head-on. He not only successfully carried out all his duties while injecting the insulin but also conquered the tough and sturdy terrain like Leh Ladakh and Kargil on a regular basis. Hats off to his tenacity, his grit, and determination to manage all these things with absolute ease.

The only other person I know about and compare with Vikram is insulin-injecting diabetes patient Wasim Akram, the lead Pakistani bowler who, despite his diabetic condition, managed to make his place amongst the world's top bowlers.

I really treasure his friendship and wish him all the best for all his future endeavours.

Vikram, from the eyes of his son, Rohan.

Rohan calls him "Baba."

"BABA"

Few things are better said in 'quotes' than what words can 'express.' I have never been interested in superhero movies, be it Marvel, DC, etc. The reason for that was I was already living with a superhero impersonated in my house. It may sound a bit jubilant, but think from a perspective of an infant growing and watching his surroundings and his parents. What I saw in my 'baba' was nothing less than what a superhero could do.

I remember, we had recently shifted to Marzban society, and we had gone for dinner at my grandparents' house in Andheri. I would never be interested in walking, the lazy boy that I was, but when baba was around, I never had a second thought. He would tell me stories on our way back home. He is good at cricket, can speak in depth about art, be it music, acting, etc. Growing up in this environment, I thought my dad could do anything that my mom and I wanted.

The one word that completes my baba is "COMMITMENT". He has always fulfilled his promises, and to say it in Bollywood terminology, from his favourite actor Amitabh Bachchan's dialogue, "Keh diya na, basss key diya." Please don't take it in the movie context. What I want to say is that this man has honoured all his commitments. He has never shifted away from experimenting in life.

The attitude imprints that I have from him are the next thing that I would love to mention.

I don't remember the exact year, since I was too young, but Reebok shoes had launched themselves in Mumbai or maybe that was the time when baba had realised that these were among the best shoes in the market now. Till then, my world of shoes was the local Bata store in Parle Market. But baba said that now since Reebok is the best brand available, I shall wear Reebok shoes and so will my son. There is a saying in Marathi "khain tar tupashi nahitar upashi" which means I will always use the best thing that is available to me. This is what I learned from this incident.

It was not about the luxury or the fancy shoes that he bought me, but that was my first moment of exploring beyond the limited scope.

Nowadays, we see reels and trends on Instagram or TikTok, where parents show their babies things that they have never seen before. In these reels, parents show their toddlers the refrigerator, garage, take them on trails, etc. In short, they expose them to things and places they have never seen.

I should say, baba was way ahead in this trend at that time. He has always been passionate about travelling, and he always travelled with me and aai. From my childhood, I have been travelling due to baba's passion for exploring various places. But the pinnacle was when my parents surprised me with a tour to Europe.

I was studying in just 6th standard, barely exposed to geography textbooks. The only thing that kept playing in my mind was that we were going to another continent. I still remember going to school the next day and going gaga over it amongst my school friends. It was surreal for me, something that my mind could not comprehend at that time. But now, after travelling almost all of the United States of America, I know when the seed was planted in me.

Now, I shall speak about the passions that I have, and one of them is "Driving". From my childhood, I have always been fascinated by cars. At a very young age, I could identify various brands of cars from a distance. I had just turned 18, and on that birthday, I was least interested in cake cutting or any celebration with friends or family. My sole excitement was to go to the RTO office and apply for my driving licence. By that time, I had already learned how to drive a car. "Let's not go into the details of how I had managed it."

So, baba took me to BKC in our Wagener car to see how I drive. I did drive at the very first stroke, without any jerks or clutch issues. He laughed and let it go. I am sure he knew that I had already learned to drive, without anyone's knowledge. But he did not dwell deep into it and excitedly told aai how miraculously I had learned to drive in the very first attempt. That was my first boost of getting confidence in driving.

Later, what happened moved me to the core. My parents were building a bungalow in Shrivardhan (which was my maternal grandfather's native). Shrivardhan is a taluka place in the district of Raigad, and it is a 6-hour drive from Mumbai. We had to make multiple trips to and fro since we were carrying most of the material from Mumbai to build the bungalow. By now, we had upgraded from Waganer to Swift Desire. On all our trips, my parents would accompany me while I drove the car. I was barely 19 years old at that time.

There came a situation where my parents and grandparents could not leave Shrivardhan, but some material had to be brought from Mumbai. So, someone had to go to Mumbai, get the material, and come back. Our drive to Shrivardhan consisted of expressways, steep winding ghats, narrow roads through villages. I kept insisting that I could go alone and come back safely. With all the twists and turns of this journey, a teenager alone behind the driving wheel was not acceptable to my mother and both my grandparents. They all feared that I would drive rashly or in some way would hurt myself. But baba trusted me. Despite all the opposition, he gave me the car keys and said, "Call me as soon as you reach home."

I will say here that sometimes I have driven the car with speed, touched the high speed of the car. But now, when my baba had shown faith in me, I had to prove him right. I successfully managed the whole trip and after coming back to Shrivardhan, baba was so pleased that he gave his white gold ring with sapphire to me immediately as a token of appreciation.

From that day, I never looked back. I drove to Goa, in the USA I drove cross country from East Coast to West Coast, etc. But the seed of confidence was planted during my first solo trip from Shrivardhan to Mumbai and back.

I moved to the US in 2015. And this decision was influenced by baba. In 2012, we travelled to the west coast of the US. My career took a definitive path once we came back from the US. I wanted to do my higher education in this country, and I started researching on the ways to get there. So, from 2015, I have been living in the USA.

A very interesting conversation happened between me and my baba on my 25th birthday. That day he told me that from now onwards, he would stop advising me on anything and that whenever I would feel like seeking his advice, his doors would always be open. He has maintained this promise till date. With all the ups and downs that happened in my life, he did caution me, gave me guidance, but only when I asked for it. I feel this is the best parenting decision that he has taken and lived by it.

While learning to ride a bicycle, after a certain point, the child must learn to ride the cycle on his own. And for this to happen, the father must let go. My baba has done this exercise twice in life. First when I was learning to ride a bicycle, and second when I had to ride a cycle called "LIFE"

I may have made wrong decisions, fallen into lows, ridden the highs, but one thing I know for sure, I carry his genes, and no matter what I face in life, I will face it bravely and overcome it.

A big thanks to my baba for making the person I am today. I have and will always look up to you for inspiration of being an ideal father, ideal husband, and an ideal diabetic person.

Lots of love from your son.

Rohan Joshi

B.E. (Mechanical), Mumbai

M.S. in Industrial Engineering from

University of Texas, USA.

AMUL PANDIT – VIKRAM'S COUSIN

Vikram... A journey from Mischiefs to Meditation.

It was a funny scene on the train. A little chubby teenage boy was busy segregating coriander leaves from the snacks, whereas all other family members were enjoying the snacks. The aunty used all tricks of 'Saam, Daam, Dand, Bhed' to convince the boy to eat the healthy and tasty coriander, but the boy was so... you know what to call. She was the same aunty who once punished the boy by locking him inside the bathroom. A good chance of revenge for the boy. The boy was none other than our Vikram... who just turned the sixtieth page of his life.

I am four years younger than Vikram. So, I have always seen him as a vibrant young boy full of numerous adventurous ideas. Many of his ideas, when put into action, ended with some kind of blunder, either harming himself with injury or fights with neighbours... but Vikram never gave up. The surroundings also nourished his ideas. A tiny cottage-like house with reasonable ground to play in front, lots of trees in the backyard, and a well with abundant water throughout the year. No wonder Vikram, with his elder brother Vivek and other like-minded friends, mastered the art of playing on trees and swimming... His love for dogs is a topic for another essay.

He must have some secret methods of studying because his report card was always good, and he cleared his SSC Exam with a respectable percentage. One reason behind his success must be his handwriting.... It is very neat, clean, and attractive. Something that will certainly catch your attention.

A movie maniac, hardcore lover of theatrics, and a sportsman. He was a very good left-handed batsman and a classy carrom player. I am a witness to his few start-to-finish games. Had he pursued any of these trades, he easily could have been a master player. I mean it. He inherited acting and dramatic skills. Charming personality, clear voice, good sense of timing, and knowledge of folk performing arts made him a good actor. He certainly could have been successful as an actor or sportsman.

He completed his master's degree and, as per the then trend, he joined a bank where he could pursue all these interests. Gradually, as the next step of life, he married Aparna, and soon there was Rohan as the cherry on the cake. With a germ of entrepreneurship, he entered investment consultancy with a future of having his own travel agency. Life was at its best for him. But destiny had some different plans for Vikram. It did not want him to be just a happy-go-lucky man. It wanted him to be someone different.

A turning point was awaiting Vikram, and one day there was confirmation that Vikram had severe diabetes. We, as second-line family members, got the news a little late, and by that time, Vikram had absorbed the first shock. A great foodie, hardcore carnivorous person with a life within the comfort zone and with no 'Nos' had to follow an altogether different path. A big challenge to anyone and especially for a personality like Vikram.

From being aggressive to being submissive....

His health challenges were a little softer than his emotional challenges. The situation was demanding him to be an altogether different personality than what he was....

And... There was this Vikram... stabilising his mind... taking reins in control, being more receptive and ready to go green from red....

Till then all the Pedas I received were swallowed by Vikram as I do not like it. All the sweets we got while being together finally rested in Vikram's tummy. The heap of chicken bones besides his plate always used to be taller than that with mine. He had hardly eaten any green vegetables so far...and Exercise.... What does that mean?

He had a long, difficult, and most unwanted path to follow. Such a phase is very delicate. One can easily succumb to any so-called Babas and impractical and foolish ideology. But Vikram stood very strong.

After that point in time, in every visit to him, we found that Vikram was changing not by any force, but willingly and happily.

Reducing rather than quitting sugar was the most obvious thing which he did. But when I noticed that he had given up non-veg altogether, I realised that he is very serious about bringing change in his lifestyle.

From a casual stroll to regular gym hours....

From Topsy-Turvy life to a very disciplined routine....

From Meat to Green Vegetables...

Vikram is a live example of what changes a human being can bring to his own life. And all this while, not only me but no one else found him in any depressive mood. Always positive about everything. Constantly encouraging change for the better....

Moving along with globalisation, modernisation, technology. Adapting to any situation, best or worst. Never crying, never complaining.

He is an avid traveller. Very soon he will celebrate the Silver Jubilee of Ladakh visits.

He is a master investment planner and tour organiser. Full of innovative ideas in both fields.

He is a staunch believer in the power of meditation. Come what may, he will never miss his meditation time.

As per his own ideology, I wish him the most and more on his sixtieth birthday.

It has been a really amazing and inspirational journey of Vikram... from Mischiefs to Meditation.

Note: In many of his achievements, he includes her, i.e. Aparna....

POEM BY SACHIN/VARSHA RAUT (CLOSE FRIENDS)

नसती हे केवळ
रंगीत ठिपके...

प्रिय विक्रम,

हा आहे तुझ्या अंगी असणाऱ्या
विविध गुणांचा मिलाफ!

हे ठिपके आहेत
या साठ वर्षांच्या कालावधीत
तू जमवलेली बहुगुणी,
बहुरंगी, बहुढंगी माणसं!

या ठिपक्यांप्रमाणे योग्य जागी
योग्य व्यक्तीची नेमणूक करून
त्यांना एकमेकांत मिसळू न देता,
योग्य अंतरावर ठेवत,
त्यांच्यातल्या गुणांचा पूर्ण विचार करून
तुझ्या आयुष्यात त्यांना स्थान दिलंस...

त्यांची अचूक योजना करून
स्वतःच्या आयुष्याचं चित्र

काटेकोरपणे सुसंगत बनवलंस...
हे तुझं व्यवस्थापन कौशल्य!

यातल्या प्रत्येक ठिपक्याला
आयुष्यात महत्त्वाचं स्थान आहे,
आणि त्यांच्यामुळेच जीवन
केवळ सुसंगतच नव्हे,
तर सु-रंगी आणि सु-ढंगी बनलंय,
याची तुला पुरेपुर जाण आहे.

हे ठिपक्यांचं चित्र आहे
तुझ्या आयुष्याचं प्रतिक!

यापुढेही आमच्यासारख्या या
अनेक 'ठिपक्यां'ची संगत-सोबत
तुला कायम लाभो
आणि स्वकर्तृत्वासोबतच
त्यांच्या सहवासाने, सहकार्याने
तुझं जीवन उजळून जावो,
हीच तुला तुझ्या
साठाव्या वाढदिवसानिमित्त शुभेच्छा!

– वर्षा व सचिन
ऑगस्ट १४, २०२४

(TRANSLATION)

These are not just random colourful dots...

Dear Vikram

They depict unique qualities you possess.

They represent multi-faceted, diverse, and dynamic individuals you related to in the past sixty years.

You have placed each dot at its rightful place, ensuring they do not overlap. Knowing the invaluable qualities they possess, you have created a harmonious balance in your life.

This is your sheer management skill.

Each dot is significant in your life and has attributed not only to make your life harmonious but also more colourful and dynamic, which you are aware of.

This dotted Rangoli is a symbol of your life.

Many such accompanying dots, like us, will always remain with you. With self-reliance and their co-existence, your life will shine brighter.

Here's wishing you a very Happy 60th Birthday!

Varsha & Sachin Raut (our best friends)

ABHAY DIXIT – VIKRAM'S COUSIN

ही गोष्ट आहे १९७०/७१ची...त्या काळात में महिन्याच्या,दिवाळीच्या सुट्टीत आम्ही मुलं आमच्या मामा,काका,आत्यांकडे रहायला जात असू...मी ही माझ्या आत्याकडे म्हणजे विवेक/विक्रम कडे रहायला जात असे... विक्रम आणि मी साधारण एकाच वयाचे होतो, मी,विवेक आणि विश्वास तब्येतीने काडीपैलवान होतो पण विक्रम मात्र चांगला गोरा आणि गुटगुटित होता त्यामुळे तो आमच्यात उठून दिसत असे...

पुढे मी आणि विक्रमने डहाणुकर महाविद्यालयात प्रवेश घेतला... collegeमधे विक्रमच्या अंगभूत गुणांना चांगला वाव मिळाला...तो college चा carrom champion होता...त्यामुळे periods bunk करून तो सगळावेळ जिमखान्यातच पडीक असायचा...पण अभ्यासातही तितकाच sincere होता...दरवर्षी उत्तम मार्कांनी पास व्हायचा...फक्त स्वत:पुरता अभ्यास न करता इतर मित्रांनाही अभ्यासात मदत करायचा...मला आठवतंय fy b'com ला आम्हाला maths होतं...१२ वीला maths न घेतल्यामुळे मला या विषयातलं ओ का ठो काहीही कळत नव्हतं...पण विक्रमने माझ्याकडून तयारी करून घेतली म्हणून केवळ मी pass झालो...

उत्तम अभिनेता म्हणून त्याने college मधे स्वत:ची ओळख निर्माण केली होती...पुढे banket नोकरी लागल्यावर तिथेही त्याने नाटकांतून भरपूर पारितोषिकं मिळवली...

College मधे असताना तो उत्तम dance करायचा..मिथुन आणि Michael Jackson चा fan होता...हुबेहुब मिथुन सारख्या steps घेऊन नाचायचा...गंमत म्हणजे college मधे मला घरून अगदीच तुटपुंजा pocket money मिळत असे त्या पैशात खाणेपिणे,सिनेमा हे परवडत नसे...विक्रमला बेबीआत्या ब-यापैकी pocket money देत असे...त्यामुळे माझा जास्तीचा होणारा खर्चं कायम विक्रमच करत असे...दुस-यांना शक्य तितकी मदत करणे हा जो त्याचा स्वभाव आहे नां तो college पासूनच आहे..

आता तो साठी पार करतोय...सुरवातीला banket नोकरी करून नंतर ती सोडून आता स्वत:च्या व्यवसायात त्याने छानच जम बसवलाय...तो माझा भाऊ असला तरी मित्र जास्त आहे...म्हणूनच आजही जेव्हा जेव्हा आम्ही एकत्र असतो तेव्हा तेव्हा तो माझ्या अधिक जवळचा कुणीतरी आहे हे मला कायम जाणवतं...

विक्रमला साठाव्या वाढदिवसाच्या खूप शुभेच्छा...

जीवेत् शरद् शतम्....

अभय दिक्षित

(TRANSLATION)

This is the period around the years 1970-71. Those were the times when children would visit their uncle and aunt's places during vacation. Vikram is the son of my father's sister. I used to go to live in their house during vacation. Vikram and I are of the same age.

I, Vikram's elder brother Vivek, and one more cousin Vishwas, we all were very lean and thin. But Vikram was fair and very healthy, and he would always stand out from all of us. We both had taken admission in the same college, Dahanukar College of Commerce. This college would give good scope for other cultural activities also. Hence, Vikram got a good opportunity to do his inbuilt cultural activities like acting and he was a good carrom player. He would not mind bunking classes for the sake of these activities.

Despite this, he would always clear all his exams with excellent marks. He would also teach many of his friends along with his own studies. I could clear a subject like maths only because Vikram helped me. Mithun Chakraborty was his favourite actor during those days. Also, he was a big fan of Michael Jackson and would dance like him. I was not given much pocket money, but Vikram used to get good pocket money from his mother, meaning my aunt. So, most of the outside food expenses would be managed by him. More than a brother, we both are very good friends. I feel very proud of him that he left his secure job and is managing his own financial consultancy. I wish him the best of everything.

KALPANA SATHE (A VERY CLOSE FAMILY FRIEND)

हाय विक्रम, तुला शष्ठ्यब्दीपूर्तीसाठी खूप खूप शुभेच्छा. आजपर्यंत जसा बऱ्या वाईट प्रसंगांना धीराने सामोरा गेलास, तीच सकारात्मकता कायम तुझ्या ठायी राहो हीच प्रभूचरणी प्रार्थना. LIC च्या निमित्ताने आपली ओळख झाली. त्यानंतर तुझ्यातल्या नेतृत्व गुणांचा अनुभव, तुझ्या सोबत केलेल्या दोन टूर्सच्या वेळी आला. पहिल्यांदा दादा, माझ्या वडिलांची पंच्याहत्तरी साजरी करायला सिंगापूर, बँकॉक, पाटायाला गेलो होतो. आणि नंतर लेह लडाख. त्या दुर्गम प्रवासात शांत डोक्याने योग्य निर्णय घेऊन, वेगवेगळ्या वयोगट असलेल्या संपूर्ण ग्रुपला सोबत घेऊन देशप्रेमाची ज्योत सगळ्यांच्या मनात जागवलीस. 16 वर्षे होऊन गेली त्या टूरला, पण आजही मराठा रेगीमेंटमध्ये रक्षाबंधांनाचा केलेला कार्यक्रम आठवला की भरून येते. हा एक जगावेगळा अनुभव तुझ्यामुळे मिळाला. त्यानंतर CFP चा आपण केलेला अभ्यास आणि त्यात मिळवलेले यश, विसरून कसे चालेल? यात अपर्णाची तुला मिळालेली भरभक्कम साथ फारच महत्त्वाची आहे, हे तूही मान्य करशील. I must say, you both are made for each other. या जवळ जवळ 20 वर्षांच्या कालावधीत आपली कौटुंबिक मैत्री घट्ट होत गेली. अपर्णा अगदी खास मैत्रीण झाली. तुम्हा उभयतांना आणि चि. रोहनला मनःपूर्वक शुभेच्छा.

सौ. कल्पना साठे आणि परिवार.

12.09.2024.

(TRANSLATION)

Hi Vikram, wishing you a very happy 60th birthday. I have seen you facing all the challenges of life so bravely, and I pray to God to keep that positive energy always flowing through you. We met each other as LIC agents, and then over the period I could witness the leadership qualities in you on two occasions.

Once, when I brought my father along with me on your international tour to Thailand, Malaysia, and Singapore to celebrate his 75th birthday. The other one was when I came with you on your Mission Ladakh. In that terrain, I also appreciate the way you keep your cool, managing so many people of different age groups.

It's over 16 years since our Ladakh tour, but the moments of Raksha Bandhan to our soldiers still bring goosebumps to me. And how can I forget our CFP studies together? It was a wonderful experience. And in all this, Aparna has been your biggest support, and this is what you will also agree. You both are made for each other. In these 20 years, we have become such good family friends. Aparna has now become a close friend of mine.

Our whole Sathe family wishes a great life to both of you and to Rohan.

Poem by Yashasvi Sane (LLB).

Our niece (some relations just happen in life. So is our Monu (Yashaswi). She came with us on our Europe tour and just became a part of our family).

Life is so precious, yet the struggle unfolds
He's a superhero, not a muggle, untold
A bucket of kindness and compassion he keeps,
Discipline and Self-control – the path he reaps.

Through trials and storms, his spirit won't bend
With courage and strength, every wound he'll mend
In the face of darkness, he shines bright and bold
A heart of pure gold, a story to be told.

Faced the hard times, took every blow
You dealt with them all, letting your courage show
Emerging stronger, a resolute man
Proved it, be it any situation, you simply can

With grit and resolve, you've shattered each chain
Overcame every storm, embraced every pain
Your spirit unbroken, your will leads the way
A beacon of strength, come what may.

We met as strangers, you caressed me as a daughter
Your love comforts, melting every bother.
Bound by a bond that'll never depart.
Forever and always, keeping you closer to my heart.

VISHWAS SOHONI – VIKRAM'S COUSIN

प्रिय विक्रम,

लेखाची सुरवात कशी करावी हा प्रश्न मला पडलाच नाही. ऑप्शन ला तर कधीच टाकला नसता..

मी, तू, विवेक, अमूल आपण सगळे साठे मॅटरनिटी हॉस्पिटल विले पारले (पूर्व) येथे अवतार घेतला. आज ही आपण असं समजतो कि इतर घेतात तो जन्म.

इथूनच आपल्या नात्याची सुरवात झाली.

विक्रम हा मोडण्या साठीच असतो या न्यायाने तुझे हात 2 दा आणि पाय एकदा मोडला. तसंच तूला गोविंद बल्लाळ देवल आणि सनी देवल, सी डि देशमुख आणि रितेश देशमुख गोपाळ गणेश आगरकर आणि अजित आगरकर आणि टेलिफोन निगम आणि सोनू निगम ह्याच्यातला फरक तूला कळला. आणि त्याप्रमाणे आदर्श ठेऊन तू वागलास ही. हे जास्त महत्वाचं.

पैसे मेहनतीने आणि माणसं ही प्रेमाने कमवायची असतात हे ही तूला कळलं.

टक्के आणि व्याजाच्या जमान्यात तू निर्व्याज च राहिलास. आपलें विले पारले झपाट्याने बदलले तू होता तसाच राहिलास. डाएट आणि आयुष्यावरच तुझं नियंत्रण कौतुकास्पद आणि सगळ्या गोष्टी गोड मानून घ्यायची ही 65 वी कला तूला खरंच जमली.हल्ली तू चिडतोस फार किंव्हा संपर्क ही कमी करतोस असं मला फार वाटत. (फार गोड नको म्हणून हे लिहीण गरजेचं होत.) क्रिकेट कॅरम tu तू चांगलाच खेळायचास. एकदा चिडून तू कॅरमवर पाणी ओतल्याच ही आठवतंय. शाळेत डबा न खाता जाडू नावाच्या कुत्र्याच्या पिल्लाला ही विवेक आणि तू डबा खाऊ घालायचात. आणि तुम्ही येथेच्छ मार खायचात. शाळेत वझे नावाच्या तुला बाई शिकवायला होत्या. तेव्हा तू पारले टिळक विद्यालयात होतास. (ह्या काही जुन्या गमतीदार आठवणी ताज्या केल्या. अजून खूप आहेत.

तुझ्या बरोबरच्या आयुष्यात सगळ्या गोष्टी आठवण्याच्याच आहेत.

वेळी अवेळी तू मदतीला धावशील हा विश्वास मला नक्की आहे.

तुझ्या आयुष्यात तुझा रस्ता तू शोधलास. गूगल ने नाही दाखवला.

Behind every success, there is a woman तशी सौ.अपर्णा तुझ्याबरोबर आहे behind नाही हे ही कौतुकाने नमूद केल पाहिजे. तुम्हा दोघांची अमेरिकास्थित शाखा चि.रोहन ह्यांच्या आठवणी शिवाय हा लेख पूर्ण होऊ शकत नाही. तुम्हा सगळ्यांना happy आणि beautiful आयुष्य यापुढे ही लाभो.

विक्रम तूला साठाव्या वाढदिवसाच्या मनःपूर्वक शुभेच्छा.

आता तू पंचांहत्तरीचा होई पर्यंत भेटूनच बोलत राहण्याचा ही आनंद घेऊ.

आता वेळीच थांबतो. हे जरा माझ्यासाठी कठीण च आहे. पण लेखाचा प्रबंध होईल नाहीतर...

मनःपूर्वक शुभेच्छा. विश्वास सोहोनी.

(TRANSLATION)

Dear Vikram,

Our relation begins right from our birthplace. You, me, your elder brother Vivek and our cousin Amul, we all were born in the same maternity hospital of Dr Sathe in Vile Parle. And we all have lived our lives as if we are some incarnations. "Record" is a synonym of your name in Marathi. Records are meant to be broken, and, in your life, you have broken (fractured) your hand twice and your leg once.

You could distinguish between Govind Balal deoul and sunny deol, between C.D Deshmukh and Ritesh Deshmukh, between Gopal Ganesh Agarkar and Ajit Agarkar, between telephone nigam and Sonu Nigam. Hence, you always had the right role model in front of you and it is very important.

Lots of effort and slogging go into earning money and lots of love and compassion go into earing good people in your life. You have managed both these things. In this world where everything is calculated in percentage on investment, you have always loved everyone without any expectations. Our Vile Parle has changed a lot in all these years, but you have not. I highly appreciate the control that you have over your diet and your overall life. You have easily accepted life as it came to you.

Nowadays, you get irritated easily, and you don't call me often is my complaint against you. (Too much of sweet is bad, so this little bitter truth)

You were a master at cricket and carrom. Being your elder cousin, some of your childhood incidents are still in my memory. Once, in a rage of anger, you spilt water on the carrom board. You and Vivek used to share your school tiffin with a dog in the school and would get beaten up by your mother. Once I asked your class teacher if Vikram is studying well in the class, she replied, "whatever bright light you are seeing in the class is because of your brother!" Anyways, I can keep on quoting many such funny incidents but will stop here. You are the person on whom the family can vouch. You run to help anyone in need.

They say, behind every successful man, there is a woman. Here I would say Aparna is not behind you, but with you always. Also, just cannot ignore your extended branch which is in Los Angeles, USA, your dear son Rohan. All my blessings are always with all three of you, and Vikram, I wish you all the best in life on your 60th Birthday.

Till your 75th birthday, let's keep meeting in person on a regular basis...

DR. ASHWINI JOGLEKAR – ANAESTHESIOLOGIST

(VIKRAM'S SISTER-IN-LAW)

It is the 60th birthday of dear Vikram... another landmark in the fulfilling journey of his life.

Going back a few decades, we Joshis were an ultra-small family of seven wonderful people. Vikram was the first "outsider" to join this family. It is never easy to enter this bond and make yourself a part of a closely knit unit. But Vikram effortlessly managed this and proved to be the eighth wonderful person ever since.

If I were to enumerate his qualities, I would not know which one is numero uno. Be it his charming smile, enthusiastic and positive outlook towards life, strong will to fight off a nagging medical condition, commitment towards a social cause or sheer perseverance in achieving his set goals... he has them all.

I have seen Vikram as a very supportive husband and the fatherly, yet friendly relation he shares with dear Rohan is indeed special. He shares the same passion for travel as Aparna, and together they have meticulously planned and executed numerous national and international trips. He has the perfect eye for beauty and enjoys being close to nature. And I must say, his wife Aparna complements him well. Hats off to their never tiring spirit. They make a wonderful couple indeed. This wonderful gesture of having a memorable worldly appreciation for Vikram says it all.

Personally, I have received a lot of genuine appreciation from Vikram for my achievements... and that is very encouraging to go on. The trust he puts in me as a medical professional is overwhelming. He never has let his age or position in the family become an overbearing factor. I am sure he doesn't recollect, but he was the one who officially taught me to ride a scooter! (something my dad would not have done)

Though I probably never missed having a brother in my life, this "brother-in-law" has more than made up for it by sharing not only our joys and troubles but also shouldering the responsibility of caring for all the five senior members of our Joshi family. Three cheers to you, dear Vikram, for playing that important role in our lives.

Looking forward to sharing many more joyous family occasions together. Wishing the most and more today and always to the one and only Vikram Joshi...

ANURADHA PRABHUDESAI – VIKRAM'S CLOSE FRIEND

विकी,

माझा जिवलग सखा म्हणजे एक अजब रसायन!!!

गेल्या ३५ वर्षांचे आमचे सख्य!!!

टोकाचा रागीट आणि तितकाच टोकाचा प्रेमळ!!!

कधी प्रचंड कठोर तर कित्येकदा अतिशय हळवा!!!

अतिरेकी हट्टी तेवढाच शांत आणि संयमी!!!

My Friend, Philosopher, & Guide.

"तुला आर्थिक व्यवहारातील काहीही कळत नाही" (खरतर अक्कल नाही) असे माझ्या तोंडावर बिनदिक्कत सांगून माझे funds invest करणारा.."विकी", तर मी केलेल्या प्रत्येक गोष्टीचे "हे फक्त तुलाच जमते" असे दिलखुलास तोंडभरून कौतुक करणारा.."विकी". वयाने माझ्यापेक्षा ८ वर्षे लहान असूनही मी कधी निराश झाले की, माझी समजुत काढून परत मार्गावर, आणणारा, माझ्याहून मोठ्ठा होणारा.."विकी" आणि त्याच्या मागच्या पिढीच्या वैचारिक भिन्नतेला समजून घेऊन सांभाळून घेणारा, श्रावणबाळही..."विकी" च!!

बँकेच्या नाटकात, आर्थिक व्यवहारामध्ये गल्लत करणाऱ्यांना सडेतोड सुनावणारा आणि त्यात जराही सहभागी न होणारा हा मुलगा त्य गृपबरोबर स्पर्धेचे दौरे कसे काय करायचा, देव जाणे. मला ते कधीही जमले नाही. अर्थात अभिनयाची आणि भटकण्याची आवड असल्यामुळे तो त्या संधीचे सोने करायचा. आजूबाजूच्या वातावरणाता त्याला काहीही फरक पडत नसे. Very much focused!!!

बँकेत कधी त्याने काम केले का मला माहिती नाही, परंतु ब्रांच मॅनेजरपासून ते सर्व स्टाफला (मुख्यत्त्वे मैत्रिणी भरपूर असल्यामुळे) पटवून कामातून सुटका करून घेऊन स्वतःचीच कामे करण्याची मखलाशी त्याला बरोबर जमायची. "तरीके बदलो, इरादे नहीं", हा ही एक गुणच!!!

त्याच्या आयुष्याच्या २७/२८ व्या वर्षी एक अनपेक्षित वादळ आले. पण हा धक्का त्याने जिद्दीने आणि विवेकाने स्विकारला आणि "तू भी क्या याद करेगा" म्हणत त्याच्याच हातात हात घालून अत्यंतिक सकारात्मकतेने वाटचाल सुरू केली.

माझ्या प्रत्येक नवनवीन कल्पनांना, activities ना, उपक्रमांना, माझ्यातील hidden potentials ना बळ देऊन, माझ्याकडून ते पूर्णत्वास नेतांना माझ्यासोबत ठाम उभे राहून धावपळ करणारा "विकी" थकायचा पण कधीही थांबायचा नाही. "It's ok" म्हणत तो चालायचा जणू काही घडलेच नाही. गुरूनाथ, गायत्री यांनाही त्याचे अप्रूप वाटायचे. स्वतःच्या कुठल्याही त्रासाचा त्याने कधी बाऊ केला नाही.

"गम निगल जाओ और सुख बाटो", या उक्तीप्रमाणे शरीराच्या आणि मनाच्या व्यथा हृदयात दडवून ठेवत असे. आजही तेच करतो. त्यामुळे त्याचे काही 'जीवलग' दुखावतात.........असो.

"असे जगावे दुनियेमध्ये आव्हानांचे लावून अत्तर, नजर रोखूनी नजरेमध्ये आयुष्याला द्यावे उत्तर" असा हा थोडासा मुखदुर्बळ, एकांडा शिलेदार!!!

माझी गेल्या २० वर्षांतील out-of-the-box घोडदौड, आयुष्याला मिळालेली कलाटणी, सापडलेले उद्दिष्ट, वयाच्या ह्या टप्प्यावर पुण्यात नवीन घर घेण्यासाठी मारलेली उडी या

सर्व प्रवासामध्ये त्याचा silent पण सिंहाचा वाटा आहे. हे ऋण मी फेडणार नाही कारण मला त्या ऋणातच रहायचे आहे.

त्याच्या साठीनंतरच्या सफळ संपूर्ण प्रवासाला माझ्या खूप खूप शुभेच्छा!!!

"जिंदगी धूप तुम घना साया"

- अनु

A Word from the hero of this book – VIKRAM JOSHI

A few months back, Aparna suddenly started praising me for all that I had done in my life. I started thinking, "How come this lady who has been having petty fights (which every married couple has) with me throughout our married life, suddenly is now appreciating me for all the good that I had done?" Then I thought, maybe she has now started realising my worth as a husband, since I was nearing an age where the whole world would recognise me as a 'Senior Citizen'.

But suddenly one day she told me that she had documented all our life incidents since our 33-year marriage. And her dream is to write a book on my life, and she had asked Megha Bajaj to be her mentor.

For a few minutes, I was awestruck and could not digest what she said. I had complete faith in Megha, but not in Aparna. It was my first thought that, is my life so special that a book can be written on it? Will my life really inspire others?

But seeing Aparna's dedication and Megha's mentoring, this book is finally ready.

If I have to say something about myself - I have embraced a variety of challenges and opportunities in life with a deep sense of passion. While pursuing personal or professional goals, I have immersed myself fully, driven by curiosity and commitment to excellence. From a banker to an actor, to a professional insurance and mutual fund adviser, to a CFP, I have sought out the paths that excite and inspire me, always aiming to learn and grow through every experience.

My passion and love for our armed forces has been a guiding force, helping me to achieve meaningful results while staying true to what I believe in. I have been doing all this by taking regular insulin shots since the age of 28.

My dedication to keeping myself fit by doing regular exercise and a controlled diet comes from my true love for my family. And writing a book on me with the intention to inspire many diabetic people to take care of their health is an epitome of love that a wife can show towards her husband.

What else can a beautiful marriage be like...

www.ingramcontent.com/pod-product-compliance
Lightning Source LLC
LaVergne TN
LVHW091102150826
845673LV00002B/686

* 9 7 9 8 8 9 5 8 8 3 9 6 9 *